CW00584775

Wayland's Guide: Isle of Wight, Portsmouth and Dockyard. Large maps, etc. [With plates.]

Henry Wayland

Wayland's Guide: Isle of Wight, Portsmouth & Dockyard. Large maps, etc. [With plates.]
Wayland, Henry
British Library, Historical Print Editions
British Library
1890
132 p. ; 8°.
010368.r.61.

The BiblioLife Network

This project was made possible in part by the BiblioLife Network (BLN), a project aimed at addressing some of the huge challenges facing book preservationists around the world. The BLN includes libraries, library networks, archives, subject matter experts, online communities and library service providers. We believe every book ever published should be available as a high-quality print reproduction; printed on- demand anywhere in the world. This insures the ongoing accessibility of the content and helps generate sustainable revenue for the libraries and organizations that work to preserve these important materials.

The following book is in the "public domain" and represents an authentic reproduction of the text as printed by the original publisher. While we have attempted to accurately maintain the integrity of the original work, there are sometimes problems with the original book or micro-film from which the books were digitized. This can result in minor errors in reproduction. Possible imperfections include missing and blurred pages, poor pictures, markings and other reproduction issues beyond our control. Because this work is culturally important, we have made it available as part of our commitment to protecting, preserving, and promoting the world's literature.

GUIDE TO FOLD-OUTS, MAPS and OVERSIZED IMAGES

In an online database, page images do not need to conform to the size restrictions found in a printed book. When converting these images back into a printed bound book, the page sizes are standardized in ways that maintain the detail of the original. For large images, such as fold-out maps, the original page image is split into two or more pages.

Guidelines used to determine the split of oversize pages:

• Some images are split vertically; large images require vertical and horizontal splits.
• For horizontal splits, the content is split left to right.
• For vertical splits, the content is split from top to bottom.
• For both vertical and horizontal splits, the image is processed from top left to bottom right.

International
Awards.
GOLD MEDAL
London, 1885;
SILVER MEDAL
London 1884

RANDALL,
SLOPER & Co.,
MINERAL WATER
MANUFACTURERS,

Soda Water.	Potash Water.
Lemonade.	Seltzer Water
Ginger Beer.	Hop Ale.
Lithia Water.	Ginger Ale.
Orange Champagne.	
Ginger Champagne	

Can be obtained in ordinary Bottles and in Silvered Syphon Vases (for which Randall, Sloper & Co., are exclusive licenses), and are sold by the principal Chemists, Hotel Keepers and Wine Merchants in the South of England.

N.B.—Every Cork branded with Name and Address.

IMPORTERS OF NATURAL MINERAL WATERS.

OFFICE AND FACTORY:—

LANSDOWNE BUILDINGS. SOUTHAMPTON

Wayland's Guide

ISLE OF WIGHT, PORTSMOUTH & DOCKYARD.

LARGE MAPS

BASED ON THE ORDNANCE SURVEY.

ENTERED AT STATIONERS' HALL.

HENRY WAYLAND,

"Isle of Wight Times" Office, Union Street, Ryde, I.W.

AND ALL BOOKSELLERS.

ENO'S 'FRUIT SALT'

FOR Biliousness, or Sick Headache, Giddiness, Depression of Spirits, Sluggish Liver, Vomiting, Sourness of the Stomach, Heartburn, Costiveness and its evils, Impure Blood and Skin Eruptions, etc., ENO'S "FRUIT SALT" is the simplest and best remedy yet introduced. It removes by a natural means effete matter or poison from the Blood, thereby preventing and curing Boils, Carbuncles, Fevers, Feverish Skin, Erysipelas, and all epidemics, and counteracts any errors of EATING or DRINKING, or any sudden affliction or mental strain, and prevents Diarrhœa. It is a PLEASANT BEVERAGE, which supplies the want of ripe fruit, so essential to the animal economy, and may be taken as an invigorating and cooling draught under any circumstances, from infancy to old age, and may be continued for any length of time, and looked upon as being a simple product of fruit. It is impossible to overstate its value, and on that account no household ought to be without it, for by its use many disastrous results may be entirely prevented. In the nursery it is beyond praise.

CAUTION.—Examine each Bottle, and see that the Capsule is marked 'ENO'S "FRUIT SALT."' Without it, you have been imposed on by a worthless imitation.

Sold by all Chemists. Directions in sixteen languages how to prevent disease.

PREPARED ONLY AT

Eno's "Fruit Salt" Works,

Pomeroy Street, New Cross Road, London, S.E.,
By J. C. ENO'S PATENT.

London and North Western RAILWAY.

DIRECT THROUGH COMMUNICATION

BETWEEN

PORTSMOUTH, SOUTHAMPTON.

AND OTHER STATIONS ON THE

London and South Western,

AND

London, Brighton & South Coast Railways,

AND PLACES ON THE

London and North Western System.

AN IMPROVED SERVICE OF EXPRESS AND MAIL TRAINS
is in operation between

LONDON,

(Euston, Broad Street, Kensington and Victoria)

AND

Birmingham, Liverpool, Manchester,

Northampton, Leamington, Wolverhampton. Coventry,
Shrewsbury, Birkenhead. Chester, Warrington
Wigan Bolton, Leeds, Stockport,
and other Towns in the Midland and Manufacturing
Districts;
Also for SCOTLAND. IRELAND and WALES.
Passengers from Stations on the London and
South Western Railway travel VIA Waterloo,
Kensington, and Willesden Junction, and
those from Stations on the London, Brighton,
and South Coast, travel either VIA Croydon or VIA
Victoria, Kensington, and Willesden Junction.
A DIRECT SERVICE OF TRAINS from and to Victoria.
Croydon, and Waterloo Stations respectively, and
Willesden Junction is established in connection with
the London and North Western Company's Express
Trains to and from the North.
For information apply to Mr. C W. LODGE, District
Agent, London and North Western Railway Office, 12,
Oriental-place, Southampton.

London and South Western
RAILWAY.

THE DIRECT, SHORTEST, QUICKEST AND

MOST CONVENIENT ROUTE

TO AND FROM THE

ISLE OF WIGHT

Ryde, Sandown, Shanklin, Ventnor, Cowes, Newport, Yarmouth

AND LONDON.

London & Portsmouth in 2 Hours

BY SOUTH WESTERN RAILWAY.

By the Direct Portsmouth Line, passing through beautiful
Scenery. The Shortest Route.

LONDON AND STOKES BAY,

The Family Route from and to the Island

LONDON AND SOUTHAMPTON.

The Short and Direct Route to and from Cowes and Newport
LONDON LYMINGTON FOR YARMOUTH FRESHWATER & ALUM BAY
The Trains arrive at and depart from the Railway Piers at
Portsmouth. Stokes Bay, Southampton, and Lymington.
LONDON STATIONS :—Waterloo, Vauxhall, Clapham Junction,
Chelsea, West Brompton, and Kensington.
An Efficient Omnibus Service from Waterloo to all parts of the Metropolis
Trains run between Waterloo and Cannon Street, City and Char-
ing Cross every five minutes. Frequent Trains between Waterloo
or Vauxhall and Chelsea, West Brompton, Kensington,
Hammersmith, &c.
Connection at Basingstoke with the Great Western Railway
for the North, and also at Salisbury with all Lines for the West of
England.—Through Tickets are issued inclusive of all charges for
assengers and luggage.
South Western Railway Offices.—Esplanade, RYDE ; at the
Pier, COWES ; at 118, High-street, Newport (next to the Bugle);
and at Chaplin & Co.'s, High-street, VENTNOR, where every
information can be obtained.
Ask for Through Tickets by South Western Railways at the Rail-
way Stations and Piers. (By order), CHARLES SCOTTER,
General Manager, Waterloo Station London.

CONTENTS.

CONTENTS.

41 & 42, UNION STREET,

RYDE, I.W.

S. FOWLER & CO.,

SILK MERCERS,

LINEN DRAPERS & LADIES'

Outfitters,

MILLINERY,---MANTLES.

One of the Largest STOCKS in the Island to select from.

FASHIONABLE

DRESSMAKING SPECIALLY STUDIED.

Wedding Trousseaux.

Mourning Outfits.

Ball Dresses, Silk and Serge Costumes.

YACHTING AND TENNIS GOWNS,
Perfect Fit, Finish, and Style Guaranteed.

LONDON PRICES. PATTERNS FREE.

CARRIAGE PAID ON ALL PARCELS TO

ANY PART ON THE ISLAND.

S. FOWLER, & CO.

41 & 42, UNION STREET, RYDE.

Great Western Railway

DIRECT AND IMPROVED COMMUNICATION
BETWEEN
THE ISLE OF WIGHT,
Southampton and Portsmouth,
AND
Oxford, Leamington, Birmingham, Shrewsbury, Chester, Liverpool. Manchester,
South Staffordshire District, North of England, North and South Wales, &c.

An improved Service of Express and Fast Trains is in operation, and Passengers are booked through between Ryde, Portsmouth and Southampton, And the principal towns on the Great Western Railway (via Basingstoke), including :

Reading	West Bromwich	Oswestry
Oxford	Wednesbury	Chester
Banbury	Dudley	Birkenhead
Leamington	Wolverhampton	Liverpool
Warwick	Wellington	Warrington
Birmingham	Shrewsbury	Crewe
	Manchester.	

The Fares charged by the Great Western route in no case exceed those charged by any other route.

During the Summer Months, First, Second, and Third Class Tourist Tickets. are issued to RYDE, COWES, SOUTHSEA, PORTSMOUTH, and BOUNREMOUTH from the principal Great Western Stations.

For further information as to Train Service Fares, &c.. see the Company's Time Books, or apply to Mr WINTLE. 30, Oxford street. Southampton, or Messrs. A. W. WHITE & Co., Cambridge Junction, Portsmouth, and High street, Winchester

HY. LAMBERT, General Manager.

Paddington Terminus.

INTRODUCTION.

———◆———

THE ISLE OF WIGHT—which is situate opposite the coast of Hampshire (the passage from Stokes Bay, Portsea, Portsmouth and Southsea to Ryde being performed by commodious steamboats in less than half-an-hour), is, as its name implies, not of modern origin. The word "Wight" is the mediæval form of the Saxon term hwit (white), an appropriate title, seeing the number of chalk cliffs about the Island. The Romans inhabited it at a very early period, many of their nobles residing here on account of the salubrious climate. Vespasian effected its conquest—whilst holding the rank of Consular Lieutenant for Claudius Cæsar —in the year 43 of the present era, 1846 years ago. The conquerors called it Vectis, or Ictis— the great depot of the tin trade. That trade probably commenced between 200 and 300 years before the last-named date, over 2000 years ago. Heredotus says that the Phœnicians carried on a trade in tin 500 years before the Nativity of the Messiah. When Tyre and Sidon were destroyed, 332 years B.C., they pursued it alone with great tact. In the meantime a Phœnician colony from Greece—dislodged from an attempted settlement at Corsica by the Carthaginians—settled at Marseilles. They strove for a participation in

B

the lucrative trade of the tin mines, the locality
of which the Carthaginians concealed.   Pytheas,
the philosopher of Marseilles, visited Britain
about 330 B.C., and gave the first information of
it to his countrymen.   The Carthaginians, however, with their colonies along the borders of the
Mediterranean, and their efficient navy, were
masters of the ocean.   As the Marseillians could
not go to the Britons in Cornwall by sea, they
prevailed on the Britons to bring their tin to the
nearest and most commodious place of transit to
the coast of France.   This was the Isle of Wight,
the most direct route for the tin from Cornwall
to its final destination.

The Island is divided into two nearly equal
" hundreds "—the word hundred when thus
applied signifying a division or part of a territory
supposed to have originally contained 100
families.   These hundreds known as the East
and West Medene, are separated by a centrical
chain of hills and downs, one North and the
other South (the Eastern part being popularly
called " the back of the Island ") and by the
river Medina, which rises in a southerly direction
at the base of St. Catherine's hill, and flows in a
northerly direction ; at Cowes it joins the Solent.
The *strata* (a Latin word signifying beds or
layers of earth, etc.) on either side of the Solent
are identical.   It is therefore fair to conclude
that they were deposited at the same period of
time, and consequently once formed dry land.

How long ago this was it is difficult to say. History tells us that the Solent existed in the time of the Roman conquerors. The word " Solent " is of Roman origin—*solvere* " to loosen," hence we get the term solvent, abbreviated into " Solent." Geologists tell us that the Solent may, at a remote date have been fordable. The land of the Isle of Wight was in ancient time continuous with other parts of England. Even the Straits of Dover did not exist at one time, and Britain itself was a portion of the Continent of Europe. The coasts of the Solent are formed of perishable beds of clay, which being very dissoluble, are by degrees rendered solvent by the washing of the waves. It is therefore scarcely open to doubt that the portion of it west of the Southampton water and the Medina river could be crossed on foot at the time of the Romans. Diodorus Siculus, speaking of this piece of water, remarks :—" At low tide, all being dry between them and the Island, they then conveyed over in carts abundance of tin." Amongst the strata, tusks of elephants have been found side by side with evidences of human beings. Elephants are not likely to have existed with man within so circumscribed a spot as the Isle of Wight, without some intercommunication with the mainland. This adds another proof that the Solent was most probably formed within a period of human existence on the Island, which was called by the Britons *Guith*—signifying separation, giving some weight to the supposition that it was formerly connected with the mainland, but by the washing of the sea gradually disjoined from it.

In 495 of the present era—when the Romans had withdrawn their arms from Britain—the Island was reduced by Cerdic the Saxon. He routed the few native Britons who still remained here. The Saxon invasion, after 150 years spent in war and carnage, gave birth to the Heptarchy. England was then divided, for the most part, into seven kingdoms, governed by seven leaders; hence the term heptarchy, or government by seven. During this period " the pleasant hills.and the quiet valleys of the Isle of Wight were often made to run with blood." Cædwalla, King of the West Saxons, slew Edel-wach, King of the South Saxons, in whose possession this Island had been, and put the greater part of the people to death. The piratical Danes afterwards plundered the Island, and in 1052 Earl Godwin stripped the inhabitants. When William the Norman conquered this country and was crowned its King in Canterbury Cathedral, on Christmas Day, 1066, he granted almost kingly powers to William Fitz-Osborne, who, for his valour at the memorable battle of Hastings, was created Earl of Hereford, and in 1068 became the first Lord of Wight, but he had first to subdue the Island. His descendants governed the Island for about one hundred years; in consequence of their assumptions Henry the

First granted it to the Earl of Devon, and this position was retained by that family until the reign of Edward the First who purchased its regalities. The story is told that the person who sold the regalities was a lady known as Isabella de Fortibus "Lady of Wight," the lineal successor of Baldwin, fifth Earl of Devonshire and Lord of Wight. She is said to have died on the very day she decided to give up all rights to the Crown for £4,000. The title of Warden, Constable, Captain or Governor, was afterwards given to the King's representative here, but arbitrary powers were resisted by the people, and the title of Governor was dropped for some time. When resumed in 1634, it had lost its harassing power and most of its emoluments; in fact the last grant seems to have been given in 1483 to Edward de Woodville. It is true that the half demented Henry the Sixth gave the title of King of Wight to Henry Beauchamp, Duke of Warwick. In a moment of mental weakness the King placed the crown on the Duke's head; but the Duke was only King in name, as no monarch of England can confer the kingly dignity on another. Since that time the title of Governor has been honorary. Lord Eversley, who died early in the year 1889, and was Governor for many years, was succeeded in February of the same year by Prince Henry of Battenberg, who married Princess Beatrice, and is the Honorary Colonel of the Isle of Wight Volunteers.

Before the passing of the Reform Bill in 1832, the Isle of Wight sent six Members of Parliament, namely ;—Newport, two ; Yarmouth, two ; Newtown, two.   Yarmouth and Newtown were subsequently disfranchised, and Newport was deprived of one Member, leaving two Members of Parliament for the Island ; one representing the Borough of Newport, and the other the Island as a County.   Under the last great Franchise Act, of 1885, Newport was deprived of its member, and one member only now represents the whole Island as a County, although in some measure connected with the county of Hampshire, and for ecclesiastical purposes is included in the See of Winchester. It is divided into three Rural Deaneries, one in the East and one in the West Medene, each containing ten parishes. The Local Government Act of 1888 is hoped to further benefit the Island, the inhabitants being almost unanimously in favour of the Island being a separate County for the purposes of the Act.   Under the new Act the Toll Gates were abolished in March, 1889.

GUIDE
TO THE
Isle of Wight.

——o——

THE ISLE OF WIGHT is 22½ miles long, It is 13 miles wide. This latter measurement relates to the widest part of the Island—from Cowes to St. Catherine's Point. The Island has an area of 136 square miles—98,320 acres. Circumference : 60 miles. Voyage round : nearly 65 miles.

The varying hills and valleys, sea and land, open and secluded spots, render the Isle of Wight, as has been well remarked, an epitome of England.

The climate is such that the floral beauty of the Island is unequalled ; delicate plants bloom here in Winter. The atmosphere is healthful. Mid-winter is less severe than on the direct mainland, and the heat of Summer is tempered by the invigorating influence of sea-breezes. Sir Walter Scott in his work entitled " The Surgeon's Daughter," speaks of the Isle of Wight as " that beautiful Island which he who sees once never forgets, through whatever part of the world his future path may lead him. Like *Prospero's* Island: The air breathes upon us here most sweetly." Nowhere does the Spring touch with more lovely hands than in the Isle of Wight, covering the whole country with a perfect carpet of wild flowers. Nowhere does the Autumn sun light up with more gleaming splendour, the rainbow hues of the flowers, fruit and corn, etc., on whose face is revealed the hectic flush of all-consuming time, and proclaims that every green thing loves to die in bright colours ; even the vegetable cohorts march glowingly away in flaming dresses.

A great portion of the land is very productive, and on the high Downs are good sheep-walks. Formerly the Island yielded nearly seven times as much as the inhabitants consumed, and a quantity of wool was exported. The produce is now considerably limited. Much of the land has been built upon to accommodate visitors and an increased stationary population, large numbers of whom depend, in a great measure, upon the visitors for patronage. Therefore, good and bad

MOUNT PLEASANT
Boarding Establishment,

ESPLANADE and CASTLE STREET, RYDE,

This Establishment is delightfully situated, only One Minutes Walk to the Left from the Pier and Esplanade Station. It stands in its own grounds, with Garden and Lawn, facing the Sea; the Baths; and the New Promenade Gardens. Good Drawing, Library and Billard rooms. ESTABLISHED, 1872.

Manager - - - - C. T. DALE.

TERMS ON APPLICATION

S. COMDEN,
PASTRYCOOK and CONFECTIONER,
FANCY BREAD and BISCUIT BAKER,
ST. THOMAS'S SQUARE, RYDE, I.W.

Wedding, Birthday, and School Cakes to order.

Agent for Montgomeries' Patent Malt Bread, and Meaby's
TRITICUMINA (Entire Wheat Meal Bread).

Agent by appointment for Horniman's Pure Tea.

MR. FRANK GOODALL, H.M.'S. HUNTSMAN,
SAYS OF
SPRATT'S PATENT
MEAT "FIBRINE" VEGETABLE
DOG CAKES (with Beetroot).

"Royal Kennels, Ascot, February 6, 1888.

"Gentlemen,—I am very pleased to say that your PATENT MEAT DOG BISCUITS continue to give me every satisfaction. I think I can speak with some experience of them, as they have been *solely* used in the Royal Kennels for the last ten years.

"Yours truly, FRANK GOODALL."

Mr. JOHN WORTHINGTON, Fishguard, writes:

"February, 1, 1888.

"I have fed my hounds and pointers and setters and other dogs on your Cakes for years, and highly approve of them, as I have no mange in the kennel since I began to use them.

"P.S.—Mine are Otter Hounds, but I hunt foxes often in the winter."

BEWARE OF WORTHLESS IMITATIONS.

See each cake is stamped "SPRATT'S PATENT" and a "X."

Spratt's patent limited DOG MEDICINES.

Small Pamphlet on Canine Diseases Post Free.

SPRATT'S PATENT LIMITED, LONDON, S.E.

THE ALBANY
HOTEL & RESTAURANT,
PIER STREET, RYDE, I.W.

Is directly opposite the entrance to the Pier and Railway,
With good Sea View.

WINES AND SPIRITS, ALES AND STOUT

Of the best quality, on draught or in bottle.

Proprietor ...... *JAMES TAYLOR,*
FOR 18 YEARS CHEF AT THE ROYAL PIER HOTEL.

Private Room, Bed and Sitting Rooms.
A FIRST CLASS COFFEE ROOM.

Luncheons, Dinners, Teas, and Suppers, Chops and
Steaks, Soups, Fish, Entrees, Jellies, etc.,

Hot Joints from 12 till 2, and from 6 to 8.

ARTHUR S. MARLOW,

Cook and Confectioner,

19, UNION STREET,

AND

3, MELVILLE STREET, RYDE, I.W.

Glass, China, Plate, Cutlery and Linen on Hire.

BALL SUPPERS AND WEDDING BREAKFASTS SUPPLIED IN THE MOST RECHERCHE STYLE.

The Luncheon and Dining Rooms are most
Comfortably Arranged.

WINES, ALES AND STOUT.

IMPORTANT!

PROVISIONS AND GENERAL GROCERIES

OF

BEST QUALITY at LONDON PRICES,

MAY BE HAD AT THE

GROCERY STORES,

46, 47, 48, UNION STREET, RYDE.

PRICE LIST FREE ON APPLICATION.

FOREIGN

WINES AND SPIRITS,

THE FINEST IMPORTED,

WELL MATURED IN WOOD AND BOTTLE.

CLARETS FROM 12s. PER DOZEN.

MINERAL WATERS.

Romford & Burton Ales.

PRICE LIST FREE ON APPLICATION.

R. COLENUTT,

46, 47 and 48, UNION STREET, RYDE.

NEARLY OPPOSITE THE POST OFFICE.

GIBBS & GURNELL,

Family and Dispensing

CHEMISTS,

34, UNION STREET, RYDE, I.W.,

Adjoining the Post Office.

IIIIIIIIIIIIIIIIIIIIIIIIIIIIII

DÉPÔT

FOR ALL KINDS OF

NATURAL, MINERAL,

AND

𝔄𝔯𝔱𝔦𝔣𝔦𝔠𝔦𝔞𝔩 𝔚𝔞𝔱𝔢𝔯𝔰.

Manufacturers of the Celebrated

ISLE OF WIGHT BOUQUET.

SEASONS affect a large majority of the inhabitants —seeing that factories, and other industrial establishments are likely to lessen the salubrity of the Island, practically are non-existent.

— RYDE. —

THE visitor, in crossing from Portsmouth or Stokes Bay to RYDE, will see to the left a charming stretch of sloping land, wooded to the water's edge, boasting many palatial residences. Among them is St. Clare—for many years the residence of Colonel F. V. Harcourt, who was formerly M.P. for the Isle of Wight. Colonel Harcourt was a younger son of the Archbishop of York. Since the Colonel's death, Mr. Egerton Harcourt, his brother, has occupied it. The residence is castellated, and is of Gothic type, with a square tower, which may be noticed by the pedestrian. Her Majesty and the late Prince Consort repeatedly honoured St. Clare with a visit. The grounds are considered to approximate to the superb.

" Apley," the seat of the late Right Hon. Sir William Hutt, K.C.B., is one of the most magnificent of Mansions. It is now in the occupation of Sir George Hutt. The briefest description, however, would occupy very considerable space, and be an unsatisfactory substitute for a personal visit. Suffice it to say that the House was built by David Bryce, a notorious smuggler.—Near

this is St. John's House, till August, 1877, the
seat of J. P. Gassiot, Esq., who then died. Since
then it has been in the occupation of General
Carr and Mrs. Tate. On the artificial grounds
many thousands have been expended.—Below
is St. John's Park, on both sides of which are
many mansions. To the right, just west of
the pier, is the Pier Hotel, and a little farther
on the Royal Victoria Yacht Club, with battery in
front ; and the Nautilus Club. Passing the marine
villa of the late Duke of Buckingham, we come
to a mansion known as Westfield, originally
occupied by Earl Spencer. It afterwards became
the seat, until 1877, of the late Admiral Sir
Augustus Clifford, Baronet, Usher of the Black
Rod—and now the seat of Sir Spencer Robert
Clifford, Baronet. In 1860, the ex-royal family
of the French dynasty took up their residence at
this most delightful Retreat. The grounds, of
different elevations, tastefully laid out and
abounding in statuary are one of two or three of
the most beautiful to be found in the Island.
They are in the Italian style, with terraces leading to a promenade along the shore. Over the
lofty ornamental stone gateway is a beautiful
symmetrical figure of a stag, which had rivetted
the attention of thousands of visitors to the
exhibition of 1851. The Prince Consort had
passed a high enconium upon the figure. The
Queen has made an express visit to Ryde so as
to see the stag in its present position. The
gilt letters—qui si sana—(here is health), form

an appropriate motto for such a rurally pictures-que spot fanned by genial breezes from the ocean.

" Ryde House," (the residence of Sir Henry Daly)—a large white mansion in its own extensive grounds, is seen lying back from the shore, amid a mass of foliage. Dotted here and there are houses of great architectural beauty. There are towering spires, and clean, sloping, foliage-bordered streets.

This is verdurous RYDE, the prettiest, the most modernly-important and largest of the Island towns. Approaching the Pier the *voyageur* may see on his right the Motherbank, where many vessels ride at anchor. On the left stretches the outline of the coast. Before him —Ryde—" spreads itself out " on a hill " backed by fields and masses of foliage." Its appearance from the water is exceptionally unique. The Pier—which is one of the main attractions for visitors—is half-a-mile in length. It was commenced in 1813. It was opened in 1814. Military and other bands play here during the Summer season. Railway and Tram communication now extends up to the landing stage of the steamboats. At the half-yearly meeting of the Ryde and Newport Railway Company, held in February, 1881, it was reported that the Joint Railway and Pier of the South Western and Brighton Company had been completed since the previous half-yearly Report, and the trains of this Company have been running to and from the Pier-head since October 1880. These improvements, trams with electric power, etc., have greatly tended to render Ryde as nearly as possible perfect with regard to through communication.

To the eastward of the town—in close proximity to what is known as the New Esplanade and Ornamental Grounds—a very few years ago there was an open space called " The DUVER," where had been buried the bodies of the crew washed ashore from the " Royal George," which on August the 29th, 1782, foundered off Spithead, a noted roadstead in the English Channel, situated between Portsmouth and the Isle of Wight—and said to be capable of holding 1,000 vessels in safety. Its security had obtained for it the name of " the King's Bedchamber," and it is the particular rendezvous of the British Navy. The title was an appropriate one, notwithstanding the loss of this ship, which was then the best in our fleet. In brief : she was heeled over for some caulking repairs when a gust of wind sent her further over, so that, the water getting in at her port holes, she sank, with about a thousand souls, including about three hundred women, who, with others, had crowded to the ship on her arrival. The noble vessel, with its 108 guns, and all, with but a solitary exception, perished. The visitor will call to mind Cowper's poem, " Toll for the brave," in which the catastrophe just related is described. A splendid promenade has been constructed to Apley. The wide-spreading back ground is in varying shades of green.

The work of beautifying and extending the " ornamental " improvements connected with the Esplanade and foreshore has been so carried out as to further enhance the natural beauties—and cannot but attract thereto the *elite* of wealth and fashion. The canoe lake, formed on the sea frontage, is available at all times of the tides. The depth of the water is so arranged as to do away with the fear of drowning, and affords almost continuous pleasure to the " young folks " by floating minature toy boats in safety, and the elder ones, who do not court danger, on venturing into something substantial enough to sustain their weight. The following details may be of interest.

The total area of the enclosure amounts to over nine acres. The sea wall is constructed of concrete—extending from the north end of the sluice—the foreshore in front of the College being utilised, and the carriage-way continued so as to be able to turn round at Apley slip, constituting a pleasant carriage drive round by the shore and up the slip by the College. The character of the wall prevents, as far as practicable, the sea dashing over.

The remaining portions of the enclosure consist of sloping banks, turfed and planted, with a centre of " ornamental water," about 922 feet

long, its greatest width being 200 feet, with an
area of over three acres.   A 10ft. wide footpath
is formed round the lake, with a facing of concrete next to the water—the height of such facing,
from the bottom of the lake, being on the north
side, two feet, and one foot six inches on the
south side ; three pipe conduits laid between the
lake and the sea, each fifteen inches in diameter,
with sluice valves, to admit the whole of the
water being changed as often as necessary.
Another conduit to admit fresh water from the
sluice during the winter, affords excellent space
for skating on the lake, the bottom of which
consists of clean sand having a slight inclination
towards the north.   The footpath round the lake
is about nine feet below the level of the Esplanade—each end of the lake—so far as regards the
spaces between the carriage road next the sea
and that on the inland side—being laid out as
lawns with ornamental planting, such lawns
sloping towards the lake, so as to afford those
walking on them a good view.   There is a slip-
way in the centre of the length of the new
enclosure, approaching the shore, with causeways
forming landing places for boats.   The two
groynes with steps leading from the new footpath can be utilised for landing-places.   The
parapets on the eastern or exposed sides shelter
persons using them.   The object in sloping the
20ft. outer footpath towards the sea is to give
pedestrians and those using the seats a better
view of the sea over the parapet wall.   Seats,

cross-paths, sloping banks, etc., enable pleasure takers to move about or rest at will. The shrubberies and flowers render the grounds pretty and as enjoyable as skill can make them.

Messrs. Hill and Co., Government contractors, well known in the Island, carried out these *desiderata* in the march of improvement from the designs and under the superintendence of Mr. Francis Newman, the Borough Engineer.

Ryde's title to be an independent town, separated from the parish of Newchurch, dates but a very few years back ; seventy years ago it was an insignificant village. The inconvenience of having to land and embark in small boats prevented the timid from visiting the town from the mainland. This diffculty being obviated in 1813-14, by the erection of the Pier, it soon became known and frequented as a health-resort, and when in 1829, it boasted of a population of 2,000, the first Ryde improvement Act was passed, but the qualification of the Commissioners consisted of £1,000 in houses or land. This Bricks-and-mortar Charter passed away in 1854, by having a Board of Representatives elected by the ratepayers The second Ryde Improvement Act became too limited, and Ryde, from being managed under the provisions of the Local Government Act, was in 1868, made an independent town—the Queen, by the advice of her Privy Council, having listened to the petition from the inhabitant householders, and granted a charter of Incorporation, constituting Ryde a Borough Town—according to the Act, 32nd Victoria—the same being in every way completed (erected) on the 23rd July, 1868—taking effect on the following November.

Ryde contains many fine Hotels, and numerous well furnished Lodging Houses. From the Victoria Pier there is excellent bathing. There are News Rooms, Libraries, a fine Theatre. etc., etc., in Ryde. The Theatre is most conveniently fitted up, whilst its stage machinery is more elaborate than those of many London houses.

The Town Hall Buildings are extensive and convenient. The New Town Hall is very large ; The Old Town Hall is at the end of the New one, and by opening large doors can be thrown into the large one when special occasions require. At the back of the Old Hall is the Council Chamber, Committee Room, etc. Below, there is the Magistrates' Hall, commodious Offices for the Town Clerk, etc., a Market-house, etc. There is a handsome illuminated clock, with four faces, in the centre of the block : this clock was presented to the town by Miss Player, who occupied Ryde House for some time. In the upper part of the town the Isle of Wight Infirmary is situated. It was erected in 1845, by the exertions of Dr. Dodd, by subscription. Its internal accommodation has been considerably enlarged within a recent date. On Thursday, February 7th, 1889, Her Majesty the Queen, accompanied

Royal Pier Hotel,

RYDE, ISLE OF WIGHT.

Beautifully Situated; Adjoining the Pier, and directly Facing the Sea, with PRIVATE GARDEN extending to the Sea.

THIS HOTEL has been entirely Re-modelled, Re-decorated, and Re-furnished. Various alterations have been made, greatly adding to the comfort and convenience of Visitors. The large Dining Room, the Drawing Room, the Smoking Room, all the Private Sitting Rooms, and the greater number of the Bedrooms command splendid Sea Views. No trouble or expense has been spared to make this Hotel homely, pleasant, and attractive.

The Four-in-hand Coaches,
(FIRST PRIZE 1886-7-8-9),

Which leave the Hotel daily during the Season, returning in time for the Table d'Hôte Dinner, are the best appointed in the Island. Seats booked at the Hotel Office.

—CARRIAGES—

Of Every Description can be engaged, and all information respecting the charming Drives and Walks in the Island can be obtained at the Office.

RYDE is by far the most convenient Centre for visiting all Places of Interest on the Island.

ALFRED E. JUPE,

25, UNION STREET, RYDE, I.W.

General & Furnishing

IRONMONGER,

SPORTS WAREHOUSEMAN, &c.

CRICKET & TENNIS GOODS

IN GREAT VARIETY.

YACHT ROPES AND FITTINGS.

TRAVELLING TRUNKS, GLADSTONE BAGS, &c.

BATHS, PERAMBUTATORS & SEWING MACHINES

For Sale or Hire.

Estimates given for Work of every description.

---

9 & 10, PIER STREET & 25, HIGH STREET, RYDE.

E. HOOPER & SON,

Fishmonger, Poulterer, and Dealer in Game.

'LIVE RIVER SALMON IN SEASON, VENISON, &c.
A Constant Supply of Ice always on hand, sent to any part of the Country.
Native Oysters, Dried Fish, Wild Fowl, &c.
Fish from all parts of England and Channel Islands.

Country Orders Punctually Attended to.

J. E. VARDY,

WINE, SPIRIT, AND CIGAR MERCHANT,

HIGH STREET, RYDE, ISLE OF WIGHT.

STAR HOTEL, SECOND CLASS HOTEL,

Chops and Steaks on the shortest notice.

GOOD ACCOMMODATION FOR VISITORS.

Five minutes walk from the Pier and from the Railway Station.

Horses and Carriages of all Descriptions.
Large Brakes start daily to all parts of the Island at 10 a.m.

London, Brighton and South Coast Railway,
The Direct Mid-Sussex Line.

The Shortest and Quickest Main Line Route to the City and the West End of London.

Boats from Ryde and also from Cowes, connecting with East Trains Direct to London Bridge and Victoria. (The City and West End Stations.)

The Best Route also, via Victoria, to the Northern and Midland Districts.

Special Facilities for the Comfort and Convenience of Families.

The ONLY ROUTE from Portsmouth to the City and West End of London without change of carriage.

Through Tickets issued and Luggage Registered including all charges.

London Stations.

London Bridge, Victoria, Kensington, West Brompton, Chelsea, Clapham Junction, New Cross, Deptford, Rotherhithe, Wapping, Old Kent Road, Peckham, Denmark Hill, Tulse Hill, Brixton, &c.

VICTORIA Station connects with the London and North Western, Great Western, Great Northern, Midland, North-London, Chatham and Dover, and Metropolitan Railways.

LONDON BRIDGE connects with the Charing Cross, Cannon Street, South Eastern Railway, and South and East London Stations.

Booking and Enquiry Offices—Ryde, The Pier; Messrs Curtiss and Son's, Esplanade; Messrs Pickford and Co's the Quay and Union-street; Ventnor, Messrs Pickford and Co's High street, and Messrs Curtiss and Son's. Springhill, The Isle of Wight Railway Stations. Newport: Railway Station, the Company's Office, High-street (adjoining the Bugle Hotel); and Cowes, the Company's Office on the Pier, where every information can be obtained. Ask for through Tickets by South Coast Railway.

London Bridge Station.   A. SARLE, Sec. and Genl. Manag

GEORGE RANDS,

BOOT AND SHOE MAKER,

25, CROSS STREET, RYDE.

A Large Assortment of Gents., Ladies', and
Children's Boots and Shoes
always in stock.

*BOOTS AND SHOES MADE TO ORDER. FANCY
SLIPPERS CAREFULLY MADE UP.*

REPAIRS NEATLY EXECUTED.

NOTE THE ADDRESS:
25, CROSS STREET, RYDE.

ESTABLISHED 1852.

WILLIAM LOCKE, & SON,

WHOLESALE & RETAIL

PORK BUTCHERS,

Sausage Makers, etc.

169, HIGH STREET, RYDE, I.W.

Fine home cured Pork, Hams, Chaps,
and Lard.

Families waited on daily. All orders punctually
attended to,

by Princess Beatrice, the Empress Frederick
and her two daughters, privately inspected the
Institution and opened a new wing. The town
is well supplied with good water. There is a
fine School of Art in George Street.—The
foundation stone of the building was laid by
the Dowager Empress of Germany,
(our Princess Royal), and the School was
opened by Her Royal Highness the Princess
Louise (Marchioness of Lorne). Here, too, is a
small Museum. The Young Men's Christian
Association, with numerous branches of labour,
has a large and suitable building in Lind Street.
Somewhat connected with it is " Hazelwood," a
large red brick erection at Swanmore, in the
upper part of Ryde. It is a home of rest and
recreation for commercial young men—many
hundreds of whom have come from all parts of
the country, and returned with renewed health
and strength. The Church of England Working
Men's Institute have premises in Star Street.
There are two Political Clubs, the Liberal Club
in High Street, and the Conservative Club in
Lind Street. There are also two capital Rowing
Clubs. The Ryde Sports and Amusements
Association arrange various Shows during the
season. The Grand Annual Regatta of the
Royal Victoria Yacht Club takes place in
August ,and attracts all the best yachts and thousands of visitors. The Town Regatta usually
takes place in August or September. Ryde has
several splendid Churches and Chapels ; the

times of service are given further on. The
Parish Church (All Saints), is a large, and, in-
ternally, a very handsome erection, belonging to
the medial period of the decorative Gothic, a
style of architecture with high and sharply-
pointed arches—clustered columns. The foundation stone was laid in 1869, by Her Royal
Highness Princess Christian. The edifice was
designed by the late Sir Gilbert Scott, with its
grand reredos, pulpit, pavement, etc. The
Organ is one of the finest in the South of England, costing £1700. The Font is of Alabaster
and has four figures representing the four rivers
of Paradise ; it cost £100. The amount was
collected on the Thanksgiving Day for the
recovery of the Prince of Wales. The Spire is
173 feet high, and cost nearly £3000. Holy
Trinity Church is also a large and handsome
building. The interior of St. James's is handsome and commodious. St. Thomas', a proprietary Chapel-of-Ease, is of a plainer character,
but the work carried on in connection with it
fills a religious hiatus in the town. St. John's
Church supplies a suburb of Ryde.

St. Marie's Church (R. Catholic), is a handsome Church in the High Street ; It was built
in 1846, in accordance with the style of architecture known as Early English. The Countess of
Clare paid out of her own purse the entire cost
of its erection. Over the altar is a magnificent
picture portraying the crucifixion with SS. Mary

and John, said to be copied from the celebrated painting in the Sistine Chapel at Rome. The ecstasy of genius, so visible in the grand picture at Moorfields, is here seen budding forth. Another picture attracts attention, namely, " The Annunciation," or the tidings brought by the angel to the B.V.M. of the Incarnation—and in commemoration of which a festival is celebrated on March 25th, popularly designated Lady-day.

The Ryde School Board have erected very large and handsome buildings in St. John's Road, and also at Bettesworth Road, for the accommodation of the children of the Borough. A large building has been erected by Mr. Alderman Barrow, J.P., in Bennett Street, intended to be used principally as a Gymnasium and Racquet Court.

Ryde is especially favoured as a honeymoon resort amongst the aristocrary, whilst English and Foreign Royalty have paid visits to the town. In 1871, the King of the Belgians was here ; so also in the same year was the Grand Duke Constantine, brother to the late Emperor of Russia, a visitor here.

The population of Ryde is about 16,000, as St. John's, Oakfield and Haylands may fairly be taken as a part of Ryde, although not included in the Borough boundary.

C 2

Walks from Ryde.

1.—The following is a very pretty walk : Along the Esplanade, and path, by the sea, past St. Clare, Puckpool Battery, etc., to the village of Spring Vale. Turn round the Battery into lanes, (look behind), keeping to the right hand turnings and watching guide posts, back into Ryde by the Park.

2.—For a short walk go along the Esplanade and continue to Sir William Hutt's private Pier. Turn up by the Lodge house, and keep straight on past a right turn, up a picturesque lane partly overhung with trees, till you reach the high road. Turn to the right into the Park and Ryde.

3.—Along the Esplanade, and passing Spring Vale, turn up a lane, and bear to the right back into Ryde.

4.—Along the Esplanade, and passing Spring Vale, keep along the shore to Sea View, and on along fine sands to Priory and St. Helen's Bays and Brading Haven. Thence to Brading. Ferry across and mount St. Helen's Village. Go to the left for St. Helen's Church—a by road from which leads to the Priory. Go on then by Nettlestone Green and Fairy Hill, (seat of W. A. Glynn, Esq.), and cross the fields to Spring Vale—returning either by road or by water side. (See above).

5.—To Bembridge as in No. 4. Instead of ferrying go on to Whitecliffe Bay and Culver Cliffs. Up Bembridge Down, the fort at the summit is Bembridge Fort, and near the cliff edge is Red Cliff Fort, Yaverland Fort is just below, and Sandown Fort is on the beach. Go down to Yaverland, and by a lane, charmingly overhung by leafy trees, to Yarbridge. To the right into Brading, and by the high road into Ryde.

6.—From the upper part of Ryde and *via* Play Street, (which anyone will direct you to), and Coppin Hall to Haven Street. Ask for Brook's Heath, and return by that, Alderman Mill and Smallbrooke. Coming to Brading Road, cross it and keep down by two seats (Westridge and Westbrooke) to Sea View, and choose either the route by the sea or by the lane from Spring Vale into Ryde. This may be done in a carriage, returning by road from Spring Vale.

7.—Up St. John's Park, and along Brading Road, etc., till Whitefield Wood is reached. Go to the right through the Wood and up Ashey Down. Return to Ryde by the high road, (part chalky).

8.—Up the Park and on to Brading. Turn to the left, over the hill and to Yaverland *via* Yarbridge, and on by the foot of the Down

(Bembridge Down), to the village of Bembridge ferry across, and return as in No. 4.—St. Helens, Nettlestone, Spring Vale. If the walk be too long, visitors can ride or drive, but must return from Bembridge by the road they came.

9.—From High Street or Union Street, along Lind Street (by the Town Hall), down West Street and to the left into Spencer Road (passing the late Sir W. Clifford's beautiful grounds). At the end of the charming Spencer Road avenue, turn down a pretty narrow path (instead of going out into the High Road), and come to Binstead Church. On to the Ruins of Quarr Abbey, now occupied as a farm house and buildings ; but the fragments of the boundary walls and other portions of ruins speak of other days. The Abbey was founded in 1132, by Baldwin de Redvers, Earl of Devon, and is said to be the first house of Cistercian monks established in England. The Abbey became the resting place of many persons of distinction, and is rich in antiquarian lore, and, by the permission of the tenant the ruins may be inspected. Go through the copse till you reach the High road, by which return to Ryde.

10.—By No. 6, or by the High Road to Quarr, and on to Wootton. Scale the Hill to the Old Rectory, turn to the left, and to Wootton Church. Cross a field path to Palmers's Farm, go through Brock's coppice, and Whippingham Road, on to

Osborne. Go down East Cowes Park, keeping to the left of the Castle, to the Ferry, by which cross to West Cowes. Return to East Cowes, and return *via* Whippingham Church, and into the Newport Road *via* Newport and Wootton. Equestrians may do this—about 17 miles.

11.—From Ryde to Wootton, return to Binstead and in lieu of keeping on the High Road, turning to the right at Kite Hill, go through Firestone coppice, across the meadows to Haven Street, and *via* Pound Farm into Ryde.

12.—Ryde to Wootton, take the road to the left to Arreton, and by the Down to Newchurch. Return by Knighton (where there is the ruin of an ancient manor house), cross Ashey Down, leaving Ryde Waterworks on the right, and to Ryde.—The Ryde Waterworks are of an extensive character and would well repay a special visit.

13.—From Ryde to Brading and Sandown by the High Road, and *via* Lake, through Cheverton to Apse, and Appuldurcombe (house and park), on to Godshill, and return through Horringford and Newchurch ; or, leaving Newchurch to the south-east, *via* Hazely to Knighton, (where there is another and larger branch of the Ryde Waterworks), and Ashey to Ryde.

14.—By the road to Brading, Sandown, and to Shanklin. In returning go to " America," by Apse farm and heath to Queen Bower, and *via* Newchurch, Knighton, and Ashey to Ryde.

15.—To Shanklin. Cross Shanklin Down to Wroxall Down, by Span Farm to Whitwell, and the Village of St. Lawrence, and by Steephill Castle to Ventnor. Return to Ryde by train.

16.—There are numerous short and pretty walks from Ryde beyond the above, little rounds that the tourist can make for himself.

Well appointed excursion coaches start daily during the season from the Esplanade to Brading, Sandown, Shanklin Chine, Bonchurch and Ventnor; also to Binstead, Wootton, Whippingham, Osborne, Newport, and Carisbrooke Castle.

The following are circular drives from Ryde, which will be found useful :—

Ashey Down and Brading ; Ashey Down and Roman Villa ; Arreton and Sandown ; Brading. Bembridge and St. Helens ; Binstead, Quarr, Fishbourne, and Newnham ; Firestone Woods ; Haven Street, Down End, Ashey Down ; Newport and Carisbrooke Castle ; Quarr Abbey and Fishbourne, Roman Villa ; Spring Vale and Westridge ; Spring Vale, Westridge and Upton ; Sea View and St. Helens ; Whitefield Woods ; Wootton, Woodside, and Newnham ; Wootton Common and Haven Street ; Whippingham Church, Osborne and East Cowes.

Places of Worship,—Ryde.

NAME.	MORN.	AFTN.	EVN.
All Saints' Church	11.0	3.45	7.0
St. Thomas's Church	11.0	3.0	
Holy Trinity	11.0	3.0	6.30
St. James's Church	11.0	3.30	6.30
St. John's Church	11.0	3.30	6.30
St. Michael and All Angels ...	10.30	3.30	7.0
St. Marie's Church, (R.C.) ...	11.0	3.0	
Congregational Church ...	11.0	—	6.30
Wesleyan	11.0	—	6 30
Baptist Church, George Street	11.0	—	6.30
Park Road Chapel, (Baptist) ...	11.0	—	6.30
Primitive Methodist	11.0	—	6.30
Bible Christian	11.0	—	6.30

RANDALL & CO.,

Soda Water	SODA WATER	Lemonade
Potash Water		Ginger Ale
Seltzer Water	MANUFACTURERS,	Ginger Beer
Aerated Water	RYDE.	Tonic Water
Lithia Water	....	Lime Water

WHOLESALE ONLY.

17, HIGH STREET, RYDE,

(Opposite Mr. DIMMICK'S, Florist,)

W. EVANS & CO.,

General Drapers, Milliners
and DRESS MAKERS.

....

SPECIALITY:

Permanent Dye Serges which do not change colour by the Sun, Sea Water, or the strongest solution of Soda, highly recommended for wear.

Post orders receive immediate attention, and sent carriage paid to any part of the Island.

TO VISITORS

Requiring Cheap and Well-made Clothing

GO TO

ARTHUR PAGE,

38, HIGH STREET, RYDE, I.W.

THE CHEAPEST SHOP FOR
*MEN'S SUITS AND EVERY DESCRIPTION OF
JUVENILE CLOTHING.*
A SUPERIOR CLASS OF CLOTHING
MADE TO MEASURE.

*A Large Stock of STRAW HATS, FELT HATS,
YACHTING CAPS and HOSIERY.*

All Goods marked in Plain Figures at Cash Prices.

The 'Atlantic' Blend,

PER 2S. POUND.

The "Atlantic Blend," is specially adapted
to the Water of the Island.

ATLANTIC TEA STORES.

116, HIGH STREET, RYDE.

AGENT FOR

KENNAWAY & CO.,

WINE AND SPIRIT MERCHANTS,

ESTABLISHED 1743.

PRICE LISTS ON APPLICATION.

AJAX & CO.,

FAMILY BUTCHERS,

39, HIGH STREET, RYDE.

MEAT SENT TO ALL PARTS OF THE NEIGHBOURHOOD
DAILY,
OF THE PRIMEST QUALITY.

THE READY MONEY

DRAPERY AND MILLINERY

ESTABLISHMENT,

T. C. BLACKETT,

No. 37, HIGH STREET, RYDE.

LADIES' AND CHILDREN'S UNDERCLOTHING,
BABY LINEN, UMBRELLAS, &c.,
*ALL GOODS MARKED IN PLAIN FIGURES
AT THE LOWEST POSSIBLE PRICES.*

Small Profits.   Sterling Value.

T. C. BLACKETT does not profess to Sell the Lowest Priced
Goods that can be had (which are always worthless and dear at
any price), but Sells at all times GOOD SUBSTANTIAL GOODS,
at the LOWEST Remunerative Prices, SUCH AS ARE SURE TO
GIVE SATISFACTION, and bring Customers back again.

A. JAMES & CO,
(LATE G. CAWS),

Tailors & Yachting Outfitters,

26, High street, Ryde,
ISLE OF WIGHT.

ESTABLISHED 1840.

A. HOLMES,

CLOTHIER, HATTER,

Hosier and Outfitter,

171, HIGH STREET, RYDE,

AND AT EAST STREET, CHICHESTER.

Clothing of Every Description for Immediate Use or to Measure.

G. A. BLACKALL,

RYDE SUPPLY STORES,

36, SWANMORE ROAD, RYDE.

GENERAL ORDERS ARE SOLICITED.

AND

SUPPLIED AT PRICES QUOTED IN ANY STORE BOOK

OR PRICE LIST PUBLISHED OF TO-DAYS DATE.

SPECIAL INDO—CEYLON BLEND—**2**s. per lb.

Hackney Carriage Fares.—Ryde.

The following are the Hackney Carriage Fares fixed by the Ryde Town Council and sanctioned by the Local Government Board :—

FARES BY TIME.

PERIODS OF TIME.	Carriage drawn by two horses.	Carriage drawn by one horse or by two ponies or mules.	Carriage drawn by one pony or mule or by two asses.	Carriage drawn by one ass.	Carriage drawn by two goats or one goat.	Carriage drawn or propelled by hand.
If the time does not exceed one hour..............	4s. 0d.	3s. 0d.	2s. 0d.	1s. 6d.	1s. 6d.	2s. 0d.
If the time exceed one hour; for each quarter of an hour afterwards.............	1s. 0d.	6d.	6d.	4d.	4d.	6d.
For any period of less than 15 minutes which is over and above any number of periods of 15 minutes completed	6d.	6d.	6d.	4d.	4d.	6d.

FARES FOR DISTANCES.

For every carriage drawn by a horse or horses, and hired for the conveyance thereon of not more than two persons and a quantity of luggage not exceeding 56lbs. in weight.

Hackney Carriage Fares (continued.)

For any distance travelled within the several parts of the Borough hereinafter described that is to say—

On the East side—The area comprised within the boundary of the Borough and extending from the Railway Station to the sea shore.

On the North—The area comprised within the boundary of the Borough extending as far west as Pelham Field, and including the whole of Pelham Field and Spencer Road.

On the West—The area extending from and including West-street as far South as Green-street.

On the South—The area extending from and including Green-street and St. John's-road and the Railway Station, ONE SHILLING.

For any distance travelled within any part of the Borough not before described, ONE SHILLING AND SIXPENCE.

For each additional person in addition to each of the above mentioned fare. SIXPENCE.

Return Fares, one half of the sums before described.

Excess Luggage Sixpence for every half-hundred-weight or fractonal part thereof over and above 56lbs.

THE GENERAL REGULATIONS.

For Hackney Carriages are as follows:—

Drivers are prohibited from smoking when driving for hire except with permission of the fare.

Drivers must not call or otherwise importune any person to hire their carriages.

Drivers will not be required to travel at a pace exceeding four miles per hour, when engaged by time.

Every Driver must wear a badge when plying for hire.

No Driver to ply for hire before 6.0 a.m., or after 10 p.m.

Every driver must produce a copy of the Bye Laws when requested by any person employing him.

No greater number than five persons. exclusive of the driver, shall be conveyed in or upon any carriage drawn by one horse or two ponies; by one pony, three persons. Two children under the age of ten years to be regarded as one person.

Check strings must be provided for all closed carriages, or carriages capable of being closed, in order to enable a person to communicate with the driver from the interior.

Tables of Fares must be affixed inside of each carriage

Any property left in any carriage must be deposited at the Police Station within twenty-four hours after it is found. If the property is of under five pounds value, the driver may demand from the person hiring the carriage an amount equal to his loss of time in taking the same to the police Station. If the property is of greater value than five pounds, the driver may demand an amount equal to one shilling in the pound; but in no case shall he receive a greater amount than twenty pounds.

Every proprietor or driver of a hackney carriage is liable to a penalty not exceeding £5 for every infringement of the Bye Laws.

GENERAL LIFE & FIRE ASSURANCE COMPANY

ESTABLISHED 1837.

LIFE—FIRE—ANNUITIES.

103. CANNON STREET, LONDON, E.C.

FIRE INSURANCES.

BUILDINGS—Brick or Stone buildings standing alone or separate from other buildings by party-walls of brick or stone, and covered with tiles, slate, or metal, provided no hazardous trade be carried on, nor hazardous goods deposited therein.

GOODS.—HouseholdGoods in private residences, and Merchandise and Stock not of a hazardous description, in buildings such as above described.

Premium 1s. 6d. per cent. per annum, with certain exceptions.

Losses by explosion of gas are made good by this Company.

Losses from Fire occasioned by lightning are made good by this Company.

Losses are paid immediately on proof, without deduction of discount.

ENDOWMENT ASSURANCES.

The Annual Premium to secure £100 to a person on his attaining the age of 65, 55, or 50; or, in the event of his dying previously, to secure the like sum to his family.

LOANS on PERSONAL SECURITY.

Loans on Mortgage Repayable by Instalments during a term of years:—Loans on Reversions and Life Interests.

AGENT FOR THE ISLE OF WIGHT:

H. WAYLAND, Union Street, Ryde

BEER IN BOTTLE.

WHITBREAD & CO.'S

London Cooper and Family Ale

3s.

London Stout and Pale Ale,

3s. 6d.

IMPERIAL PINTS, CORKED OR SCREW STOPPERED.

AGENTS FOR

NEWPORT:— JORDAN AND STANLEY, 3, St. James's-square; C. M. CHIVERTON, The Mall.

RYDE.— HENRY ADAMS, 3, High-street; J. N. TARRANT. 36, Union-street and High-street; WATSON BROS., Sea View, MR E. G. STROUD, 19, Cross-st.; A. & J. DRANSFIELD, 77, Union-st, H. SPANNER, 2, Pier street.

SHANKLIN:- DEAR AND SONS, High-street.
SANDOWN: - S. J. HABGOOD, Osborne House, Fitzroy-street.
VENTNOR:—DEAR AND SONS, High-street; J. BRIDDON, Esplanade; P. OWEN, 34, High street, H. CRUTCHLEY, The Volunteer.
COWES:—DEAR & MORGAN, 91 & 92, High street,
FRESHWATER:—R. LEVER, Post office, School green.

ROBT. BAKER, Sole Agent,
277, Gray's Inn Road, London W.C.

All these Beers are brewed by Whitbread and Co., at Chiswell street, London, E.C., and bottled by them at their stores, 277, Gray's Inn Road, London, W.C.

Distances and Census.

	Miles from Ryde.	Miles from Newport.	Miles from W. Cowes.		Miles from Ryde.	Miles from Newport.	Miles from W. Cowes.
Alum Bay	20	13	16	Needles	21	14	18
Appuldurcombe	10	6½	11½	Newchurch	6	5½	10
Arreton	7½	4	9	Newport	7	—	5
Ashey	4	5	10	Newtown	12	5	10
Bembridge	8	11	16	Niton	15	8½	13½
Binstead	1	6	11	Osborne	7½	4	1
Blackgang	16	9½	14½	Parkhurst	8	1	4
Bonchurch	11¼	10½	15	Sandown	6	9	14
Brading	4	7	12	Sandrock	16½	10	15
Brixton	14	7	14	Shanklin	8½	10	15
Brook	17	10	15	St. Helens	4	11	16
Carisbrooke	8	1	6	Ventnor	12	10	16
Calbourne	12	5	10	Whippingham	6	3	2
Chale	16	9	14	Wootton Bridge	3	4	5¼
Cowes, West	8	5	—	Yarmouth	17	10¼	12
Cowes, East	8	5					
Freshwater Gate	18	11	15				
Godshill	1	5½	10½				
Lake	7	8	13				
Mottistone	12	9	14				

Miles

Ryde is distant from London 79
Newport ,, ,, ,, 86
Cowes ,, ,, ,, 82
Ventnor ,, ,, ,, 92

Parishes.	1881	1871	Parishes.	1881	1871
Arreton	1920	1910	Niton	801	732
Binstead	813	748	Northwood	8175	7374
Bonchurch	670	641	Ryde	12670	12576
Brading	7918	5648	St. Helens	4343	3112
Brixton	530	641	St. Lawrence	249	135
Brooke	195	183	St. Nicholas	351	273
Calbourne	693	644	Shalfleet	1053	1195
Carisbrooke	8305	8198	Shanklin	1780	1432
Chale	681	652	Shorwell	622	633
Freshwater	2754	2638	Thorley	189	144
Gatcombe	228	249	Ventnor	5684	4841
Godshill	1302	1197	Whippingham	4578	3730
Kingstone	69	66	Whitwell	706	666
Mottistone	143	140	Wootton	104	82
Newchurch	1356	985	Yarmouth	779	806
Newport	3233	3556	Yaverland	153	118

The population of Ryde is about 16,000, as St. John's, Oakfield, and Haylands may fairly be taken as a part of the town of Ryde, although not included in the Borough boundary.

BRADING.

FROM Ryde to Brading. The Church, which
is dedicated to St. Mary, is said to be
nearly 1200 years old, its foundation stone having been laid in the year 704 through the pious
instrumentality of Wilfred, Bishop of Winchester;
but no authentic view of any portion of its
architecture has ever been given further than
its being chiefly Transition-Norman in style—
though that was not in vogue in 704. It consists
of a chancel (separated by a Norman arch)
chancel-aisles, nave and aisles, The roof is supported by massive Norman pillars. The arches
on each side of the middle aisle are fine and
ancient ; but in modern times, until 1865, they
were covered with white-wash ; in that year the
edifice was "restored" at the cost of Sir Henry
Oglander (deceased) and Lady Oglander. There
is an old stately early English tower, standing
on four arches forming the western porch, sur—
mounted with a spire, rebuilt at the beginning of
this century. The Oglander chapel is at the east
end of the south aisle, and contains some very
interesting tombs and monuments—one to the
left near the altar, having kneeling effigies, and
an inscription commemorative of a wife and son
of a Sir "Oglander," who lived nearly 500 years
ago. The altar-table is of the date of Queen
Elizabeth, and within the rails is a curious and
elaborately-engraved slab, with an effigy of a
Knight—to Sir John Cher-win (Curwen),

Governor of Porchester Castle : the side work is supposed to represent the twelve Apostles : it was originally inlaid with silver. The altar tombs of Sir William Oglander, and Sir John Oglander, his son (Lieutenant of the Island and Lieutenant-Governor of Portsmouth, who died in 1655, aged 70), are in the splendid Oglander Chapel (south aisle). Here also is the tomb of Sir Henry Oglander, who died in 1874. A fine east window has been placed in the chancel by his widow, Lady Oglander. The Oglander family can trace their residence in the Island for over 800 years—their ancestors having come over with William the Norman. They settled at Nunwell ever since the time of the Conquest in 1066. The widow of the deputy-steward of Brading has a lock of the hair of the Dairyman's Daughter, well authenticated.

The parish of Brading is the largest in the Island, comprising 10,107 acres. "Ye Kyng's Towne of Bradinge" (so named from its early Saxon settlers, the Bradingas) is an old Corporate town, controlled by a senior and a junior bailiff, a recorder, and thirteen jurats. Near the Church is a new Market-house, with Town Hall over, which is an exact copy of the old structure, and under the block is an old pair of stocks—disused. The rings observed in some of the very old houses were used on some of the festivals to support some of the tapestry decorations. There is only one street,

and at about the middle of it is an open space
with a large iron ring (the bull ring), in the
ground.   Here, in former days, bull-baiting was
practised.   In a lane to the right, at the bottom
of the hill, is the " Young Cottager's cottage."

The Rev. Canon Clayton, writing from Sandown to his parishioners at Stanhope, on the
19th February, 1881, said that on Wednesday,
February 16th, " We had a remarkably fine day.
The sun shone all day long in a cloudless sky,
although on the same day in London there was
so dense a fog that gas was kept burning in the
houses and shops.   We took advantage of the
weather to walk to Brading, that we might see
both the Church in which good Mr. Leigh Richmond used to preach, and also the gravestone of
the Young Cottager, whose most instructive life
Mr. Leigh Richmond wrote.   We called on the
Vicar, whom I knew some years ago at Cambridge.   He kindly took us into the Church and
explained all about the parish as it was and as
it is.   Adjoining the Church we saw a kind of
Court-house ; and in it we saw, (what I believe
was to be seen in Stanhope some years ago, a
most forbidding looking instrument of punish-
ment called " The Stocks," with its padlock and
chains.   There it stood ready for immediate use
upon any drunkard or other notorious transgres-
sor.   Near it was also a whipping post.   But
we were most interested in the Church-yard.
In Stanhope we have a gravestone recording the

death of some one aged 101. We saw in Brading one recording a death of 102 years of age.
Near this were the two tombstones which, eighty-
three years ago so much interested little Jane,
" The Young Cottager." On those two tombstones the inscriptions are :—

> Forgive, blest shade, the tributary tear,
>   That mourns thy exit from a world like this ;
> Forgive the wish that would have kept thee here,
>   And stayed thy progress to the seat of bliss.
>
> No more confined to grovelling scenes of night,
>   No more a tenant pent in mortal clay :
> Now should we rather hail thy glorious flight,
>   And trace thy journey to the realms of day.

These lines to the memory of Mrs. Berry,
have been set to music by Dr. Calcott, and are
known wherever English music is cultivated :—

> "It must be so. Our father Adam's fall,
> And disobedience, brought this lot on all,
> All die in him—but hopeless should we be,
> Blest Revelation ! was it not for thee,
> Hail, Glorious Gospel ! Heavenly light, whereby
> We live with comfort, and with comfort die ;
> And view, beyond this gloomy scene, the tomb,
> A life of endless happiness to come.

At the east end of the chancel stands the
tombstone erected to the memory of Jane herself.
That inscription is as follows :—

SACRED TO THE MEMORY OF

LITTLE JANE,

WHO DIED 30TH JANUARY, 1799,

IN THE 15TH YEAR OF HER AGE.

Ye, who the power of God delight to trace,
And mark with joy each monument of grace,
Tread lightly o'er this grave as ye explore
The short and simple annals of the poor.
A child reposes underneath the sod,
A child to memory dear, and dear to God ;
Rejoice ! Yet shed the sympathetic tear:
Jane, "The Young Cottager," lies buried here.

The silly and destructive custom of writing names on everything visited by thoughtless tourists, at one time covered Little Jane's tombstone. In a lane at the bottom of the hill, stands the cottage in which Little Jane lived and died.

The Brading Harbour Company have succeeded in reclaiming 850 acres from the encroachment of the sea. There is a railway from Brading to St. Helens and Bembridge, affording the visitor every facility for visiting these places.

The Roman Villa near Brading.

This Villa is situated at Morton between Brading and Sandown.

It is easily accessible by road and rail—from every part of the Isle of Wight.

This vast collection of antiquities lay over fourteen hundred years, unknown and unsuspected, within a foot or two of the top soil—which was almost yearly disturbed by the plough until within the last ten years.

KANGRA VALLEY INDIAN TEA GROWERS ASSOCIATION.

FRENCH & LANGDALE,

14, ST. DUSTAN'S HILL, LONDON, E.C.

PACKED IN 1lb, ½lb, and ¼lb TINFOIL LINED PACKETS.

GUARANTEED TO BE ABSOLUTELY PURE AS SUPPLIED IN INDIA.

TRADE MARK ON EVERY PACKET.

No 1 ORANGE PEKOE   4/- lb

,, 2 PEKOE   3,- lb

,, 3 PEKOE SOUCHONG 2/6 lb

TERMS :—

CASH WITH ORDER;

Nine Pounds delivered Free per Parcels Post;
Twenty Pounds and upwards Carriage Paid to any Railway Station.

Reductions of 1d. per lb if 20 lbs taken, and 2d. per lb if 50 lbs taken.

Tasting Samples gratis by post of any kind named.

AGENTS' TERMS ON APPLICATION.

Money order payable to

FRENCH AND LANGDALE,

LOWER THAMES STREET.

The Isle of Wight Times

IS THE

BEST LOCAL PAPER.

Sent to any part of the Isle of Wight & Hampshire for
THREE HALF-PENCE.

Wayland's Time Tables

For the Isle of Wight, All Parts of England, the Continent, &c., ONE PENNY, Post Free, THREE HALF-PENCE.

WAYLAND'S GUIDE

To the Isle of Wight contains a LARGE MAP, based on the Ordnance Survey.

POST FREE ONE SHILLING.

A Shilling Spent in Wayland's Guide to the Isle of Wight, will save many a Shilling to visitors, Who desire to see the beauties of the Island.

WAYLAND'S GUIDE TO RYDE,

With LARGE MAP,

POST FREE 3 d.

Wayland's Voyage

Round the Isle of Wight—POST FREE THREE-PENCE.

HENRY WAYLAND,

"ISLE OF WIGHT TIMES" OFFICE, UNION-ST., RYDE, AND ALL BOOKSELLERS.

DR. J. COLLIS BROWNE'S CHLORODYNE.

THE ORIGINAL AND ONLY GENUINE.

ADVICE TO INVALIDS.—If you wish to obtain quiet refreshing sleep, free from Headache, relief from pain and anguish, to calm and assuage the weary achings of protracted disease, invigorate the nervous media and regulate the circulating system of the body, you will provide yourself with that marvellous remedy discovered by Dr. J. COLLIS BROWNE (Member of the College of Physicians, London), to which he gave the name of

CHLORODYNE.

and which is admitted by the Profession to be the most wonderful and valuable remedy ever discovered.

CHLORODYNE is the best remedy known for Coughs, Consumption, Bronchitis, and Asthma.

CHLORODYNE effectually checks and arrests those too often fatal diseases—Diptheria, Croup, and Ague.

CHLORODYNE acts like a charm in Diarrhœa and is the only specific in Cholera and Dysentery.

CHLORODYNE effectually cuts short all attacks of Epilepsy, Hysteria, Palpitation, and Spasms.

CHLORODYNE is the only palliative in Neuralgia, Rheumatism, Gout, Cancer, Toothache, &c.

*** From Lord Francis Conyngham, Mount Charles, Donegal, December 11th, 1868.

Lord Francis Conyngham, who this time last year bought some of Dr. J. Collis Browne's Chlorodyne from Mr Daven port, and has found it a wonderful medicine, will be glad to have half-a-dozen bottles sent at once to the above address.

*** Earl Russell communicated to the College of Physicians that he had received a despatch from Her Majesty's Consul at Manilla, to the effect that Cholera had been raging fearfully, and that the ONLY REMEDY of any service was CHLORODYNE.—See *Lancet*, Dec. 31st, 1864.

CAUTION—BEWARE OF PIRACY AND IMITATIONS.

Caution.— Vice-Chancellor Sir W. Page Wood, stated that Dr. J. Collis Browne was undoubtedly the inventor of CHLORODYNE; that the story of the defendant Freeman was deliberately untrue, and which he regretted to say had been sworn to.— See *Times*, 13th July, 1864.

Sold in Bottles at 1s. 1½d., 2s. 9d., and 4s. 6d. None is genuine without the words, "Dr. J. COLLIS BROWNE'S CHLORODYNE" on Government Stamp. Overwhelming Medical Testimony accompanies each bottle.

SOLE MANUFACTURER

J. L. Davenport, 33, Great Russel-street, Bloomsbury, London.

REFRESHMENT ROOMS,

1, UNION STREET, RYDE,

(CORNER OF PIER STREET),

LATE HIGH STREET, NEWPORT.

L. K. GARRETT,

(LATE HARVEY),

COOK

AND

Ornamental Confectioner,

FANCY BREAD AND BISCUIT BAKER.

Novelties a Specialite !   Cakes a Specialite !   Pastry a Specialite !

The Cheapest and Best House for Cakes of all kinds.

SCHOOL, BIRTHDAY, and CHRISTENING CAKES TO ORDER.

RICH ALMOND ICED BRIDE CAKES,

Artistically Ornamented, from 1s. per lb.

ONLY THE BEST AND PUREST INGREDIENTS USED.

FRENCH, SWISS and ENGLISH PASTRY, CAKES, &c., &c.

Home-Baked Bread, Coburg, Milk, Vienna and
Wheaten Digestive Bread.

SCOTCH and FRENCH MUFFINS and HOT ROLLS

EVERY MORNING.

A Good Selection of Novelties—Foreign Fancy Goods, **Fancy
Boxes** and Baskets of Pure Confectionery and Chocolate from **the
Best Makers.**

*Choice Wines, Dublin Stout, Bass's and Allsopp's Burton
Ales on draught and in bottle.*

The first "find" was that of a tile, when a survey was taken in 1854; but until three or four years ago nothing of importance was done.

Diggings under proper supervision, have been carried on in earnest, and proofs that this Villa was occupied by a Roman of rank and fortune are undoubted; but we will not trouble our readers by quoting the customs of the luxurious Romans.

Upon entering the property, the visitor should be careful to examine the coins at one corner—and also to walk outside and see the old Roman style of ventilation and distributing heat.

The Chambers are as annexed :

1.—Stags' horns and a variety of bones, with a few tiles.

2.—Black and Caistor pottery ; also Samian ; a few faced stones, nails, bones, etc.

3.—The first piece of pavement discovered (15ft. 6in. by 17ft. 6in.), represents two gladiators fighting. One of them is armed with a trident—a spear with three prongs, as represented in the hand of Neptune, the mythic god of the sea—and also of " Britannia," pictured as holding control of the ocean, seen on English bronze coinage. The other combatant has a net. The central portion of the pavement represents

D

a house with a kind of a dome or cupola ; also
a fox under what looks to be a grape-vine.
Time, and perhaps, the occasional bringing to
the surface of a portion of the work by some
agricultural implement, may have something to
do with the fact that the other portion of the
subject is destroyed. The most curious panel is
on the south side, consisting of a man with the
head and legs of a cock, standing in front of a
small house, with a flight of steps leading up to
it ; on the right are two winged griffins. Here
can be seen the head of a Bacchante—a priestess
or one who joined in the celebration of the feast
of Bacchus, the mythic god of wine and revelry.

4.—Similar to No. 2. Here was found a
quantity of articles, such as iron lamp-hook,
hinge and vitrified stones—or stones converted
into glass.

5.—In this chamber the walls were about
eighteen inches in thickness, and the pavements
of grey marl tesseræ—or six-sided die. No
special comment is here needed.

6.—Here was a colonnade fifty feet in length.
The subject of the pavement is the god Orpheus,
seated and wearing a red Phrygian cap, playing
a lyre, by which he attracts various animals.

7.—Entrance to this out of No. 4 ; being
divided by the hedge, and the tesseræ injured by
fire, attracts little notice.

8.—Similar remarks apply to No. 8 as to No. 7. The half-circular formation, consisting of Bembridge stone, lined with mortar of a salmon colour, was probably used as a furnace for baking.

9.—Nearly twenty feet square, paved with red and white tesseræ, in good preservation.

10.—Number of red flat tiles on the floor. The green glass evidences the presence of glass-smelting at this spot.

11.—Rough concrete floor.

12.—Finest room yet excavated; thirty-nine feet six inches by twelve feet in the western portion; fifteen feet six inches in the eastern portion. Solid masonry projections, squared and cut, divide the room. From the projections curtains were hung, dividing one portion of the apartment from the other. There is a group of figures at the east end. The head of Medusa in the central circular medallion is recognised by her locks, consisting of a nimbus of snakes. Of the four medallions (two figures each) one represents Ceres—the fabled goddess of corn; in another can be seen Arethusa and Alpheus, (the river god.) The third one depicts Hercules and the Queen of Lydia, to whom he is giving the double-headed axe which he had taken from the Amazons, a race of sanguinary female warriors.

D 2

In the fourth is Dauphis with his Phrygian cap, pandean pipe and shepherd's crook ; a pastoral nymph is here enjoying a dance ; four heads of Mercury (the winged messenger of gods), are seen—two blowing straight trumpets and two on the couch ; these are allegorical of the four winds. Between the two quadrangles is seen Hipparchus, the father of astronomy ; astronomical instruments are by his side. At the west end of the chamber the four seasons are symbolized. The plumage of the peacock, pecking at a vase of flowers, is beautifully worked in colours. The closely wrapped figure holding in her left hand a leafless bough and a dead bird, represents winter. The mythic story of Perseus and Adromeda is depicted. In the ornamental margin is represented sea tritons and mermaids. One border is terminated by the Swashtika of the Buddhist, or Greek Archaic cross.

13.—This was probably a recess entering into an arbour or garden ; here there may have been a bath.

14.—A small chamber with concrete floor. The remnants of the walls show that the Romans were not ignorant of the art of imitation marbling.

15.—The " hypocaust " or warming chamber. It contains fifty-four pillars of tiles arranged upon a floor of cobble stone ; two feet six inches high ; thirteen tiles each. Furnace and hearth stones are exposed to view, as also the two heating flues.

16.—Floor paved with concrete ; walls coloured red ; patches now remain.

17.—Also concrete floor ; plaster walls covered with blue, splashed with black and red. Here were found many rich and rare specimens of antiquities.

18.—Here we see that in the early part of this era the practice of splashing the wall, in imitation of marble was in vogue. In this decade of the eighteenth century we have imitation marble papers on our walls.

19, 20 and 21.—Are of little interest to the visitor.

22.—A large chamber in the centre of the northern wing—fifty-four feet by twenty-one feet ten inches ; floor of rough concrete ; here were found pieces of bronze and shells.

23.—Thirty-nine feet eight inches by thirty-two feet ; foundation three feet thick. This chamber seems to have been used as a barn.

24, 25, 26 and 27.—Are of no great interest to the casual visitor.

28.—Here is situated the well, four feet three inches in diameter and seventy-eight feet deep. It was filled with rubbish, and the skeleton of a man was discovered.

29.—A chamber on the east of the well house and separated.

30.—Here, as in No. 29, was found a block of stones.

This is reputed to be the finest Roman Villa in England.

Places of Worship.—Brading.

	MORN.	EVEN.
St. Mary's Church	11.0	6.0
Congregational Church	10.30	6.0
Bible Christian Chapel	10.30	6.0

SPRING VALE, SEA VIEW, &c.

PASSING Ryde Esplanade and Apley, and keeping to the shore, within a short distance is SPRING VALE—which, sixty years ago, was a sandy desert of furze and bushes. It is now quite transformed. It is a pretty spot, and being only two miles from Ryde, is frequented by visitors during the summer season. On account of the broad and firm sands it affords great bathing facilities, and advantage is taken of its position in this respect. Bathing machines are provided for the accommodation of the public.

Just beyond Spring Vale are the houses known as SALTERNS—which, though now unused as Salterns, were one hundred years ago in full play with all the apparatus for salt boiling. Salt was then a guinea a bushel, and the industry was a productive one. This, and the " Seafield House," the property of the late Henry Beach, Esq., was the work of James Kirkpatrick, Esq. This gentleman, with his family, did a great deal of good amongst the community.

After passing Sea Field we arrive at what was formerly known as Old Fort, but now designated

SEA VIEW.

It is a quiet pleasant resort, distant from Ryde Pier, in a direct line, a little over two miles. It has a charming sea bathing position. As a place of residence the oldest inhabitant can remember when it had not been evolved from the matrix of time—beyond the fact of a few individuals making their stay there. Sea View may be said to date from about the year 1807, when three families took up their permanent abode here. One of the first businesses was, of course, that of a baker and confectioner—the *cause* for this being, that though man cannot live by bread alone, yet " bread is the staff of life." During the last few years, however, some large buildings have been erected. There need not be *ennui* for lack of society. At the same time, those who desire quietness can have it at Sea View.

Sea View was built in the year 1807, standing on two and a half acres of land, which with some additions to it shortly afterwards, raised the area to four acres. It was in possession of one family by exchange with the proprietor of the Fairy Hill estate. With but few exceptions it remains in their possession to the present time ; their profession is that of pilotage. They have followed this calling over one hundred years. Not one of the original family (Caws) ever lost a ship or a life in their charge. About fifty years ago the proprietor of Fairy Hill enlarged the area of Sea View, by letting off on long leases, a portion of his estate. Since that time many great additions have been made. We might mention the residence built by Le Marchant Thomas Le Marchant, Esq.—now in the occupation of Henry Thomas Barclay Esq. Some members of the Barclay family have largely patronized Sea View for nearly fifty years. They now make it their summer residence. They have a pleasure yacht here.

Sea View proper has had no case of criminal conviction ever recorded against it. Habits of sobriety on a specific basis were introduced here more than fifty years ago.

The beach at Sea View has long been considered unrivalled for its beauty, and a new feature of attraction has been added to the Bay in the shape of a " SUSPENSION PIER," running off about 1,000 feet into the sea. It springs from a little esplanade, bounded by a newly-erected sea wall.

This Suspension Pier is composed of fine gracefully arched spans, supported by galvanized steel wire cables running over four standards (or towers "), formed by eight groups of four piles each. Each of the three middle spans are two hundred feet long. The two end spans are each about one hundred and forty feet in length. Several new principles not hitherto adopted, have been introduced in the construction. The timber piles and framing are well creosoted, and the deck is preserved by Mr. Kyan's process—which consists of impregnating the wood with a pre-peration of mercury. The entire construction is exceptionally unique. Although there is a charming airy lightness about the entire structure, yet perfect safety is undoubted. It may be mentioned, in passing, that this Pier has with-stood, without the slightest injury, some of the severest gales that have ever been known upon this coast, including the great snowstorm of January 18th, 1881. This fact is the more noticeable seeing that the fabric was not com-pleted at that period, and, as a consequence, any weakness at any part would then have been detected. This proves the utility of employing a series of iron rollers—the weight being de-signed to be equally borne on each span. The Pier is rendered very attractive as a promenade by having numerous alcoved seats (sheltered from the winds), at intervals—and a little pavilion at the Pier head. A native of the Island—Mr. Francis Edward Caws, C.E., of Sunderland—designed and erected the structure, which supplies a long felt want of the inhabitants. Boats and steamers can embark or disembark at any state of the tide from the Pier. A series of steps have been arranged so as to avoid the inconveniences often attendant upon getting out of or entering boats, etc.

A short and pleasant road leads up from the Pier to the commercial part of Sea View.

The Church—or, more correctly speaking, the Proprietary Chapel—was erected by voluntary contributions in 1859. It is built in the Gothic style of architecture. There is a nave and north aisle. The pastoral care is deputed to the Vicar of St. Helens.

There are two places of worship of the Methodist persuasion—Wesleyan Methodism having been introduced as early as 1810.

ST. HELENS.

ON the high road, about a mile from the village of Nettlestone, is St. Helens—the approach to which commands extensive views of the Channel. The houses constituting St.

Helens are situated on a rising ground, forming a square, with the Green in the centre. In the neighbourhood are a number of gentlemen's seats. St. Helens is four miles south-east from Ryde, and ten miles east from Newport. The ancient Church of St. Helens stood on the Duver at the entrance of Brading Haven; but the sea having made considerable encroachments, the edifice had to be abandoned. The waves carried out the work of submerging the church until the tower only remained. This tower has been strengthened with solid masonry to serve as a mark for vessels entering St. Helens Roads. The Church, consecrated by Bishop Trelawney, in 1719, was considerably enlarged on and improved in 1829. It was, for the causes stated, rebuilt in 1831, in a more elevated position. It is a stone building of the Gothic type, with red brick facings. It is not of an imposing character. Not far from the remains of the old church is a mansion standing in the midst of a fine wood, through which pleasant walks have been formed to the water-side. It is designated "The Priory" from its having been founded in the year 1155 as a Priory for Cluniac Monks— one of a reformed order of Benedictine Monks. They were so called from *Cluni* in Burgundy. The Priory was what is known among *religieuse* as a monastic cell, in connection with an Abbey in Normandy. Henry VI. appropriated the property, and it was used by him for the building and endowment of Eton College. Sir Nash

Grose, Judge of the Court of Queen's Bench was a former owner. Miss Gladstone who died at Cologne, in January, 1880, was a former resident at the Priory. Henley Grose Smith, Esq., Lord of the Manor, now occupies the charming spot.

BEMBRIDGE.

WITHIN an easy walk of Brading is the quiet peninsula—three miles in length—at the extremity of which Bembridge is situated. It has the appearance of being separate and different in character from the rest of the Island. Here ploughing is done by ox-teams, the animals being harnessed with collars—as in Gloucestershire—and not driven in bows and yokes, which is according to Sussex fashion.

The pretty village of Bembridge was in 1827, formed into an Ecclesiastical district — the population of which was, in 1871, 862. The Church of Holy Trinity is built of stone. Its architecture is Early English. It consists of a chancel, nave, south aisle, and north and south porches.

At the south-eastern portion of Bembridge Down are the CULVER CLIFFS—at the west end of which is a cavern known as " Hermits Hole." At the top of the cliffs is a splendid obelisk. It was raised in the year 1849, by the members of the Royal Yacht Squadron, to the memory of Earl Yarborough, who was their first Commodore.

The term " Culvers " originated from the fact that formerly large quantities of pigeons used to select the place as their home. The word culver is an old-fashioned term for the wood-pigeon.

All the coast from Bembridge to Whitecliff is pretty : but the glory of the district is Whitecliff Bay—one of the most secluded and delicious spots in the whole Island. This is the place to spend a long summer's day—to walk or bathe — with the smooth, tide-swept sands at one's feet —or to bask in the sunshine upon the sweet scented turf which crowns the noble cliff at the southern end of the Bay.

BINSTEAD AND QUARR.

BINSTEAD is a parish and village on the coast one mile west from Ryde. It is reached by passing through the gates at the end of Spencer Road, and along a pleasant footpath. It is separated from the parish of Ryde by a small stream running into the Solent. After crossing this bridged-over stream we see the small Church of the Holy Cross. This antique Church (restored in 1862) is in the early English style. A chancel, nave and north aisle were added in

1876.　There is a bell-turret.　We may, in truth, call this an English village Church.　The Churchyard has the appearance of being the " God's acre " of many of our ancestors. The lettering on numbers of the tombstones is obliterated by old time.　The interior of the building is worth observing.　The reading desk is supported by a figure of Moses, with arms upheld by Aaron and Hur.　These well preserved carved oak figures, with their Hebrew type of countenance, carry the mind of the Bible student back to those days when " God came from Teman, and the Holy One from Mount Paran."　The font represents Eve's Temptation, the Expulsion from Eden, the Doom of Labour, Death, Christ's Baptism, Crucifixion, Ascension,—and the last Judgement. The comparatively new stained-glass window has for its representative subject " The Good Shepherd," given by the former Rector, the Rev. Philip Hewitt, who recently died, having had charge of the Church for about half-a-century.　A tablet to the aged Pastor's memory has been placed in the Church by the congregation.　Passing out of the edifice and Churchyard the attention of the visitor is directed to the private entrance of the latter.　Over the gateway is preserved an old Norman door, with a curious piece of sculpture, the rude outlines of which have been so worn away by time as to render it difficult to decipher for what it is intended.　It was formerly over the south door.

At the last restoration it was placed, together
with the arch, in its present position. The
grotesque figure is designated the IDOL. Carefully tracing the few outlines still remaining, there
appears the dim contour of something like the
figure of a man seated on a ram's head. This
was intended by the ancient inhabitants of this
Island to represent Thor as a-Thor). Thor was
one of the principal deities of the Scandinavian
mythology. He was the eldest son of Freiga
and Odin, the greatest of the Scandinavian
heroes, who lived 70 years B.C. in Denmark.
He was a monarch, priest, and poet, and after
his death was regarded by his countrymen as a
god. To Odin, *i.e.* Woden, the fourth day of
the week was consecrated ; hence, Woden's-day
(Wednesday). Friega (or Frida) was the
Norseman's Venus, to whom the sixth day of the
week—Friday (Frida's day)—was consecrated.
Our Scandinavian and Saxon ancestor's believed
in the world being governed by gods and god-
desses, and they had a superstitious respect for
ghosts. We might instance in later times the
phantom warning given to Wallenstein, the
shadowy apparition re-visiting the glimpses of
the moon in *Hamlet*, or the spectral shapes that
torment the sleep of Macbeth. Amongst the
Angles, Jutes, Danes and Saxons, every day had
its deity. Thor was supposed to reign over the
aerial regions, in a palace composed of 540 halls.
He directed the meteors, winds, and storms.
He launched the thunder and pointed the light-

ning.   To him the Saxons and Danes prayed
when requiring favourable winds, rains and
plentiful seasons.   The fifth day of the week,
Thursday (Thor's day), was dedicated to him.
The fact of this idol being placed over the
entrance of the original building, suggests that
the neighbourhood was frequented in very early
ages.   The upper limestone found here has been
quarried at least from the time of William I.
The material of a Roman altar, discovered at
Winchester, very much resembles the stone at
Binstead and Quarr.   Mr Roach Smith has
stated if it could be positively ascertained to be
identical it would prove that the quarry was
worked several centuries earlier than alleged.
Geologists and masons are of opinion that they
are identical.

During a summer evening the walk from
Binstead to Quarr is enchanting.   A very
pleasant green lane from the Ryde and Newport
Road leads to the ruins of the Abbey.   The
walk through the copse to Quarr, sheltered from
the glare of fervent light is lovely.   At the end
of a narrow winding path is an open piece of
ground.   Here stands the remnants of QUARR
ABBEY, dedicated to St. Mary Magdalen.   It
was founded in 1132-4 by Baldwin de Redvers,
who was created Lord of Wight.   It was
endowed with the Manor of Arreton.   The
Monks were of the Cistercian Order (White
Friars)—reformed Benedictines.   These Monks

were zealous and skilled workers in agriculture. They brought much of the ground of the vale of Newchurch into cultivation. Lord Redvers (who was buried in the Abbey Chapel) and other lords, added to the endowment, until the greater portion of the best land of the Island belonged to the Abbey. Edward III. granted a license in 1340, to the then ruling Abbot. By the powers granted, the Abbey was fortified by a strong wall surrounding it. Some idea of the strength of this wall may now be gathered from its ruins. The original circuit enclosed an area of forty acres. Time would not have destroyed the erection for another 1000 years. It, however, came under the veto of Henry VIII. On its suppression as a religious house, it was purchased by the brothers Mills, (John and George.) These two wealthy Southampton merchants dismantled the greater portion of the buildings. Sir Thomas Fleming (Lord Chief Justice of England), purchased the estate from the representatives of Mrs. D. Mills. This nobleman continued the work of demolition. It eventually came into the hands of Mr. J. B. W. Fleming, of Stoneham Park. The Abbey site is occupied by a farm house and out-buildings. The materials for these erections are alleged to have been obtained from the ruins. The large barn used to be the Refectory. Just over the doorway is the stone framework of a three-light window. It has, however, been blocked up. The ivy-covered outer walls, in connection with the shell of one

E

of the buildings standing in a meadow on the east side of the farmhouse, have a picturesque appearance. In 1867, some labourers, employed in making a road through the Abbey grounds, came upon three small stone chests. These chests contained three human skeletons. They are supposed to be the remains of Count Baldwin, his wife, and son Henry. It was evident that they had been removed from the place of their original burial. At a short distance south of the ruins of the Abbey is a wood. It was designated "Eleanor's Grove." This name originated from a tradition that Eleanor of Giuenne was buried here. This lady was the wife of Henry II. The weird "story of long ago" is, that she was imprisoned at Quarr, where she died and was buried in a golden coffin with magical rites. Those who have striven to gain possession of the coffin are said to have thus been prevented from securing it. It is rumoured in entering the kind of vault and pushing open the door, the "three birds of omen strange" tapped with their beaks on the lid, and the awed intruder just observed a passing glance of the golden coffin descending into the cavernous depths. History tells us that Eleanor was kept a prisoner at Winchester under Randulph de Glanville. She is said to have remained at Winchester for sixteen years, namely until the accession of Richard I. It is further stated that she was interred at Fontevrand by the side of her husband. Something, however, might have happened which historians of those days dared not state, and the truth might have been hidden in this Arabian Night's type of narration.

SANDOWN.

A PRETTY little town, which has rapidly sprung from a village to its present size and importance. Less than fifty years ago Sandown was a mere cluster of fishermen's cottages with a single inn. Near the sea are large forts mounting ten heavy guns. Large barracks are on the other side. Part of the original barracks are now used as a military hospital. In 1874 the Crown Prince and Princess of Germany, (Princess Royal of England), family and suite, resided here for a long time. A fort armed with heavy guns has also been erected. The main attraction for the general visitor is the magnificent Bay, which offers tempting inducements for boating and fishing.

The salt water at this part of the Island is strong and pure. The sands gradually shelve into the sea. Bathing is very pleasant on account of the firmness and smoothness of the sands. The atmosphere is particularly genial and salubrious. The Isle of Wight Railway Company has a station here. The line to Newport was opened in 1875. The parish Church, (Christ Church), was built in 1845-7. It is a

E 2

spacious stone building in the Early English style of architecture. It has been twice enlarged and now seats 800 persons. The pulpit is of carved oak. In this church is a memorial window commemorative of Lieutenant Boxer, R.N., one of the officers who perished in the ill-fated "Captain." The living is a perpetual curacy belonging to Brading. The foundation stone of the stone Church, at Lower Sandown, was laid by Lady Oglander, in September, 1878. There is a Local Board of Health, consisting of fifteen members, forming the Local Governing Authority of the Parish. The town is lighted with gas. It may interest visitors to know that the quiet spot of Sandham Cottage, Sandown Bay, was purchased by "Wilkes the Unquiet," from General James Barter, in the year 1788. Wilkes designated the house his villakin. The locality is remarkably healthy. The prospect is one of unbroken magnificence. There is every facility for seaside recreation.

CULVER CLIFF. Here we have a view of the magnificent white cliffs between Sandown and Bembridge. The term "Culvers" originated from the fact that formerly large quantities of pigeons used to select the place as their home. There is a cavern on the side of the Cliff—"The Hermit's Hole,"—from which there is a fine sea view. Yaverland Fort, lower down, mounts eight heavy guns; and Redcliffe fort, four 110 pounders. These, with Sandown fort, command the approach to Spithead. At Whitecliffe Bay there is a dangerous ledge of foreland.

The position of the terrace erected on the Gandaloufe estate, is all that can be desired for seaside residences. The seaside is not the only attraction in Sandown. As a health resort the figures of the Registrar General tell us that the death rate averages usually from eight to ten per thousand. In many other large towns it is over twenty per thousand. This is a proof of the salubrity of the place. On account of the situation of the town, and the nature of the soil on which it is built, there are but few days during the year when confinement to the house is necessary. This is accounted for from the fact that immediately after the heaviest rain, the moisture is absorbed by the porus earth, and walking is not only possible but healthy, and generally pleasant. The conditions of hygiene are here in such abundance that, with ordinary care, Sandown ought to be a place where old age or accident only terminate life.

SANDOWN is a word which antiquarians tell us is derived from the common suffix *down*, signifying a tract of naked and hilly country, often applied to a bank or elevation of sand thrown up by the sea. Sand Down, being abbreviated into Sandown, carries with it a self-evident etymology. Dr. Croft, however, says that it originally derived its name from Sandham, denoting the excellence and extent of its sands.

Mr. F. C. Fowler, writing from Fern Cliff, under date April 5th, 1881, speaks of the advantages of Sandown as a health resort, not being sufficiently known. His letter contains the following remarks :—" I remember that the late Mr. Smith, of Rosel, used to tell me that the result of a daily comparison of your temperature of this place with that of Reading, which he kept up with a friend there for some years, was, that ours was ten degrees the warmer in winter and ten degrees cooler in summer, or twenty degrees nearer to an equilibrium, a matter of no mean importance to an invalid."

Before leaving Sandown the visitor should see Christ Church. This edifice, with its modest spire, was erected in 1874. The building, (recently enlarged), is a good specimen of Early English architecture. Symbolical sculpture, usually seen in church buildings, is singularly absent in one respect, *i.e.*, so far as regards the position of the altar. It is a rule, with almost a few exceptions as to the grammatical one of *u* always following *q*, that the altar shall stand to the East in token of "the holy place." Entering an English Church we are supposed to face the East, with the West at our back, the South lying on the right hand, the North on the left. The opinion that the " adversary " has his stronghold in the North is a very old one, St. Austin allows that it is the result of a figure representing the evil angels, having grown torpid with an icy hardness, being adverse to the light and fervour of charity and goodness.

In the churchyard are seven graves of men of the

" EURYDICE."

The monument records the following :—" Sacred to the memory of seven brave men of Her Majesty's Navy, who lie buried here, after having first found a watery grave on Sunday, March 24th, when H.M.S. " Eurydice " foundered in a terrific squall off Sandown Bay."

The " Eurydice " was a wooden fully-rigged sailing vessel of 921 tons burthen. She was commissioned at Portsmouth in 1877 as a training ship for second class ordinary seamen, and sent to the Barbadoes station. She was built in 1843, and was at one time considered the smartest and quickest 26-gun frigate in the service. In 1877 she was converted into a training ship, as stated, at Mr. White's ship-yard in Cowes, and was completed for sea at Portsmouth Dockyard. She sailed from Portsmouth on the 13th of November, 1877, with a crew of about 300 ordinary seamen, Captain Hare and a number of officers. The vessel left Burmuda on March 6th, 1878, for Portsmouth, with about 300 persons, including supernumeraries. On Sunday, March 24th, she came in sight of the Isle of Wight. At two o'clock, when about two hours'

sail from Spithead, the weather being very fine,
the sun glinting down in all its glory, she was
seen to set her studding sails, although under a
good deal of canvas before. The beautiful
spectacle was watched by a number of people
from Shanklin and Sandown. There was a
moderate breeze, just abaft the beam. Such a
" frigate under full sail " was a rare and charming sight to nautical men. At a quarter to four
when well across Sandown Bay, a sudden and
unexpected " squall " came on, A downfall of
snow obliged all watchers from the land to seek
shelter. The squall of wind and snow was over
in half-an-hour, but during that time, the ill-
fated vessel had struck, heeled over, and went
down in seven or eight minutes. The schooner
" Emma " succeeded in saving an able seaman
named Benjamin Cuddeford, and a first class
ordinary seaman, nineteen years of age, named
Sydney Fletcher. These were the only survivors
of the disaster, and one of these, (Cuddeford),
died at Plymouth on Saturday, April 16th, 1881.
At his death it was declared that he had never
fully recovered from the shock of his long
immersion.

Dean Stanley has truly said : There was a
darkness all over the land in that fatal hour
when the " Eurydice " went down in the sight of
the harbour, carrying to the depths of the ocean
the flower of our nation. Pitilessly did the
storm do its work." The Dean went on to say

that it appeared at first to be scarcely an accident. It seemed almost the working of fate.

Bearing in mind the foregoing, there appears much truth in the statement that "Eurydice" is an unlucky name. Without debating the question of good or ill luck of names, it cannot be forgotten the first Eurydice, herself and another, died of a serpent bite, and this third, as now recorded, goes to the depths in sight of the shores of the land from which she had long been absent. Eurydice is a name borne by many women in the works of ancient writers. For instance: the wife of Amyntas, who married her uncle Aridæus, the natural son of Philip and hanged herself at the instigation of Olympius. Another bore the name, who was the wife of the poet Orpheus, who, as she fled before Aristæus, was bit by a serpent in the grass and died of the wound. Orpheus was so disconsolate that he ventured to descend into Hades, where, by the melody of his lyre, he obtained from Pluto the restoration of his wife to life, provided he did not look behind him before he came upon the earth. He violated the condition and she was taken from him for ever.

Walks from Sandown.

To Yaverland one-and-a-quarter miles by the road close to the shore, past the site of the old

Sandown Fort. A pretty walk, affording a view of Ashey, Brading and Bembridge Downs, the hamlet and fort of Yaverland, and the sea. The artist's pencil may be pleasantly employed at Yaverland.

To Bembridge, four-and-a-half miles, which embraces a fine prospect including Brading, Nunwell, Swanmore Church and a portion of Ryde; Bembridge Fort and the monument to Earl Yarborough will also be noticed. The return journey may be made along the sands and cliffs, but the distance would be increased to six miles.

To Brading two miles, Ashey, Mersley, and Arreton Downs. A walk along these Downs will afford the pedestrian a grand panorama. The journey may be performed by rail if preferred.

To Alverstone, four miles; Knighton, six miles; Newchurch, seven-and-a-half miles. Passing under the chalk quarries, there is a slight ascent, affording another splendid view. Descending to Alverstone, the botanist will find interesting specimens. It was at Knighton that Leigh Richmond had his first interview with the "Dairyman's Daughter." Passing on to Newchurch, is the mother Church of Ryde, which will be found to be one of the most ancient in the Island. The Church was built in the year 1087 by William Fitz-Osborne, a cousin of William Rufus, as an atonement for ravages committed in the New Forest, and is known as one of the churches of atonement. It is mentioned in Doomsday-book. The present edifice is believed to have been erected in the early part of the thirteenth century on the site of the previous church.* The return to Sandown may be varied by Queen's Bower and Lake.

To QUEEN'S BOWER, train to Alverstone, and thence walk across the bridge over the Yar. The return to Borthwood and Lake is a pleasant variation.

Places of Worship.—Sandown.

	Morn.	Even.
Christ Church	11.0	6.30
St. John's Church, Lower Sandown	11.0	6.30
Baptist Chapel	11.0	6.30
Wesleyan Methodist Chapel	11.0	6.30
Bible Christian Chapel	10.30	6.30
Congregational Chapel	11.0	6.30
Primitive Methodist Chapel	10.30	6.30

* There is an interesting mem. in the register:—" The Bishop of this Diocese, Sir Jonathan Trelawney came over from Gosport early in the morning on ye 27th of June, 1719, and the same day consecrated the church of St. Helens, which was built on new ground, the Church as it stood before was too much exposed to ye wash of the sea, and presently after it on ye same day he consecrated also ye chappel of Ride in this parish, being built by Mr Playor, at whose house in Ride he din'd, and went over again on the same day." On Friday, Oct. 14th, 1887, the 800th anniversary of the old Parish Church was celebrated.

SHANKLIN.

ONCE a leafy village, but now a town of some importance. As a town Shanklin is of recent growth. In the year 1846, Lord Jeffrey wrote that the village of Shanklin was small and scattery, "all mixed up with trees, and lying amongst sweet, airy falls and swells of grounds, which finally rise up behind in breezy Downs 800 feet high, and sink down in front to the edge of the varying cliffs which overhang a pretty beach of fine sand, and are approachable by a very striking wooded ravine, which they call the "Chine." Shanklin is protected from the prevailing south-west bleak winds, so searching in winter. Dr. Betts says the climate is well adapted "to restore the health and energies of those who by residence in hot climates have lost *tone* and are suffering from affections of the liver and the depressing effects of dyspepsia. It will be found particularly serviceable as a residence for weakly children." Until the Railway of the Ryde and Ventnor Company was opened, 1864, the place was so secluded that few of the general non-islanders knew of its existence. It was, therefore, up to that time, a small village of pristine appearance. In 1863 the place was included under the Local Government Act of 1858. To give some idea of the growth of the population we quote the following census items : In 1851 there were 335 inhabitants; 479 in

1861 ; in 1871 1,432. The 1881 census 2,780 ; increase in ten years 1,348. Old Shanklin retains, in a great measure, the attributes of an old English village. The cottages in summer are covered at their entrances by honeysuckles and plants that flourish well in the open air. Many of the houses of modern Shanklin present fine architectural features, being really very pretty.

The Esplanade forms a promenade and drive, protected by a sea wall 600 yards in length. A similar beach to that of the sister town of Sandown will be found here, in fact, from Sandown to Dunnose the sands, firm and broad, are the finest in the Island. The " lion " of the place is the far-famed Chine, which no one must omit seeing. Leigh Richmond gives a good description of the Chine, (a Saxon word signifying " cleft,") in his " Young Cottager." Narrow below, the chasm is about 150 feet wide at the top. The steep sides are clothed in verdure, rich underwood overhanging them. The cascade is not extraordinary, as except after heavy rains, the quantity of water is very small. The entrance to Chine Hollow is close to the " Crab " Inn. Here there is a little rustic fountain, bearing on a shield lines composed by Longfellow, author of the " Psalm of Life," commencing with the following words : " Tell me not in mournful numbers life is but an empty dream." When

Longfellow was staying at Hollier's Hotel, in 1868, he wrote the lines :—

O traveller stay thy weary feet !
Diink of this fountain, pure and sweet !
It flows for rich and poor the same.
Then go thy way, remembering still
The wayside well beneath the hill,
The cup of water in his name.

The old, or what is popularly termed, Parish Church, is dedicated to St. John, the former dedication being said to be that of St. Blaize, or Blasius, bishop and martyr. It was built as a Church of the manor in Edward the Third's reign, on the sight of a former structure dating back to the reign of Stephen. Here are several memorials of the Popham and White families.

St. Saviour's on the Cliff is a handsome stone building, gothic in style, opened in 1869. The tower contains a peal of eight bells, dedicated on the 29th of July, 1887, and supplied by Messrs. Mears and Stainbank.

The new Church of St. Paul's, Gatten, the foundation stone of which was laid on January 25th, 1875, and consecrated July 26th, 1876, is practically the Parish Church.

A Catholic Mission, consecrated to the "Sacred Heart," has been recently established here. Visitors and residents are well catered for, there being some excellent Clubs, with good tennis grounds, etc. Shanklin also boasts of a Literary and Scientific Institute.

The "Chine" inn, which was burnt down in

1869, but again erected, marks a lovely spot, the inn itself being overshadowed by a majestic oak.

Walks from Shanklin.

To Luccombe Chine, one-and-a-half miles, by shore or cliffs. In taking the former the tide must be noticed.

To Cook's Castle and Shanklin Down. Passing along the path from the churchyard through two or three fields, one of the finest prospects in the Island is presented. Cook's Castle is a modern tower, surrounded by trees, and the very place for a picnic; hot water for tea may be obtained at a cottage. The view from the top of the tower is extensive and picturesque. The return may be made by rail from Wroxall.

To Ninham, Apse, and Languard. A pleasant walk of from three to five miles. Lovers of wild flowers may revel in abundance of specimens. A pleasant variation may be enjoyed by returning *via* Lake, or going on to Sandown.

The services at the various places of worship are at the usual times.

LUCCOMBE CHINE.

LUCCOMBE CHINE—a deep ravine in the cliffs, about one hundred yards broad at its mouth, and stretching two hundred yards inland. It is a well secluded spot, with two or three fishermen's huts. It is, we think, as

attractive as that of Shanklin—and the East
End. Walk through the Landslip. Opposite
this Landslip the sad wreck of the *Underley* took
place in 1872. With reference to the name
Luccombe Chine, we have proof of the veracity
of the statement that the names of places in the
Isle of Wight are mostly of Saxon origin. The
Anglo-Saxons, as a rule, named their towns,
villages and settlements after some natural
feature of the locality indicated by the prefix or
suffix of the word. A knowledge of this fact
enables us to judge of the situation of most of
them. Thus the prefix *Comp*, as in Compton,
and the suffix *comb*, as in Luccombe, indicates
the locality to be in a valley. *Chine*, as we
before observed, signifies "cleft," a word almost
exclusively belonging to the Island, applied to
the fissures or clefts in cliffs formed by the action
of streams of water upon the wealden and green
sand strata.

BONCHURCH,

ONE of the oldest villages in the Island.
Inland the scenery is simply magnificent;
above are high walls of chalk; below, dales,
"dressed over all" in flowers. Horseshoe Bay
is within reach. Water-lilies bloom on the pond
from which a stream, picking its way among
rocks, runs, and is the base of a foliage cavern.
St. Boniface Down is 783 feet above the sea;
ascend this and be charmed with the view. Also

see St. Bonny's Well. The Pulpit Rock—a low rugged mass of cliff—400 feet above the sea, is reached by a flight of steps from near the pond. It was formerly surmounted by a flagstaff, and termed "Shakespeare's Rock." Its present name is derived from a wooden cross (enclosed) being substituted. Several literary memories linger around Bonchurch, the following having had their permanent or temporary abodes in the village; Miss Elizabeth Sewell, Rev. J. White, Leech, Richard Doyle, and Thackeray. This was also the native place of Admiral Sir Thomas Hobson, who from a common sea boy rose to be one of England's naval heroes. The story is told that Hobson was left an orphan at an early age, and was apprenticed by the parish to a tailor at Niton. He did not like the occupation. As he was one day sitting alone on the shipboard, a squadron of "men-o'-war" came round Dunnose. The whole village was attracted to the shore by the beauty of the sight. Young Hobson ran down to the beach, cast off the painter from the first boat he saw, quickly reached the Admiral's ship, entered the service as a volunteer, and turned the boat adrift. Next morning the Admiral fell in with a French squadron, and a warm action commenced. Hobson obeyed orders with alacrity, but after two hours' fighting, he became impatient and asked the sailors what was the object for which they fought. On being told they must fight till the white flag at the enemy's mast head was struck, he replied, "Oh, if that's

F

all, I'll see what I can do!" The ships being
at that moment engaged yardarm to yardarm and
obscured in the smoke of the guns, Hobson took
advantage of the circumstance. He mounted
the shrouds unperceived, walked the horse of the
mainyard, gained that of the French ship, ascended to the maintop gallant-masthead and
carried off the French flag. At the moment he
gained his own ship the British tars shouted
victory without any other cause than that the
enemy's flag had disappeared. The French
crew were panic struck, and being confused, ran
from their guns. The British seized this oppor-
tunity of boarding and taking the vessel.
Hobson descended from the shrouds with the
French flag round his arm and displayed it to
the sailors, who received the prize and Hobson
with rapture ; but some of the officers threatened
him for his audacity. The English Admiral,
however, encouraged him and ordered him to
walk the quarter-deck from that day. Hobson
successfully passed through the several ranks and
had command of the "Torbay" in the celebrated affair off Vigo. On his return he visited
his old master and mistress at Niton. They did
not recognise Jack Hobson in Admiral Hobson,
who dropped in *incognito*, until he sang a favourite
song of his apprenticeship. The pleasure of
recognition by the old lady, who had regarded
Jack with favour, was evident—for she left her
preparations and rushed into the room crying :
" It is our Jack !" The gallant Admiral did not

forget his host and hostess—but left them solid proofs of his good feeling.

The Old Church (1070-80) is worth a visit. St. Boniface is said to have landed here. The tourist should notice the remains of mural paintings, representing the Last Judgment ; and a cross, carved in black oak, which is said to have been brought here from a Norman Abbey. In the Churchyard will be found a tombstone in memory of the Rev. William Adams, who died in a house adjoining the Church. He wrote the "Religious Allegories." He was also the author of "The Shadow of the Cross." Over his tombstone—which is in good preservation— is a raised iron cross, so placed that, in reality, "the shadow of the cross" falls on the tomb. Towards the western wall is the grave of John Sterling, who lived at Hill Side, Ventnor. His great, but imperfect genius has been commemor- by Carlyle, "the Chelsea Seer," who died in March, 1881. The Churchyard is generally admitted to be one of the most lovely spots in England ; but the inconsiderateness of excursionists has caused it to be closed.—The New Church (services at 11.0 and 3.30) was erected in 1847-8. The Rev. W. Adams laid the first stone, June, 1847, but died before the consecration, December, 1848.

VENTNOR.

WHICH, though it shows to best advantage from the sea, will be found very attractive.   It was styled by Cuthbert Bede, " a sunlit town that sits basking in the lap of nature, and is mirrored by the sea."   There is a capital Esplanade, shingly beach, and pier ; looking behind, some of the most ornamental villas are seen.   The carelessness with which they would seem to have been pitched on projecting cliffs adds materially to their attractiveness.   Ventnor possesses all the accommodation of a first-class watering place.

Ventnor—now the capital of the Undercliff— was formerly, like Ryde, within the parochial limits of Newchurch.   About a quarter-of-a-century ago there were about eight or ten fishermen's cottages and a small inn—whilst the neighbourhood did not boast of a name " all to itself."   Therefore, instead of looking for the etymology of the designation of the old Celtic " Gwent" and " Nor " (referring to its position on the chalky and open shore) we shall be more likely to find it in a modification of some modern local allusion.   There are indications of the plausibility of this surmise in the fact that the original proprietor of the CRAB AND LOBSTER tavern, who held possession the greater part of last century was an ancestor of the present occupiers, and was known as the " Vintner "; he also held possession of the uniquely-located mill, so often portrayed.   This mill went by the name of the Vintner Mill—and in the course of time the bay in its vicinity was designated Vintner Cove.

In the beginning of the present century, however, Vintner Cove and Vintner Mill were called
Ventnor Cove and Ventnor Mill. Similar
changes of vowels in the pronunciation, and
eventually in the spelling of often used designa-
tions, were of frequent occurrence before the
present era of fixed orthoepical rules became so
universal among the people. Naturally, as the
houses in the neighbourhood developed into a
pleasant resort, the pretty name of Ventnor was
permanently adopted.

Ventnor Cove is terraced with villas, covered
with evergreens, and backed by the lofty Downs
which shelter the inhabitants from the "bleak
blowing blasts of Boreas," but throws back the
delectable summer breeze. The shore in the
Cove is covered with fine shingle, among which
may be found small pieces of transparent quartz.
These particles of rock crystal are designated
"Ventnor diamonds."

The renowned UNDERCLIFF, which is sheltered
from cold winds, will afford many a delightful
ramble. There will be seen the effects of the
great landslip of 1799, destroying a hundred
acres. The jagged Undercliff has a mild
climate, and is a region of singular beauty and
interest—rocks, dells, lawny slopes, leafy bowers
rugged masses of cliff, sparkling chalk, with
continuous music in the murmuring of the waves.
Facing it is the wide ocean ! The cliffs are from

600ft. to 700ft. high.   St. Boniface Down is
within an easy distance of the town.   Here
flowers display themselves, and sweet peas
bloom in December.   The Undercliff is a ledge
of land on lower cliffs (a quarter to half-a-mile
wide, extending from Luccombe to Blackgang,
eight or nine miles), with a range of towering
cliffs in the rear.   It is the result of a tremendous slip.   The decoration of Undercliff by
nature is something almost unsurpassable.

The romantic character of the Undercliff is
greatly owing to the formidable slips that have
occurred in the course of ages.   The general
stability of the place as at present constituted is
guaranteed from its having settled down into
what geologists term a state of repose.

In the neighbourhood are many places of
interest which should be visited.

The Cottage Hospital for Consumption, the
foundation stone of which was laid by the
Princess Louise, is worthy of notice.   This is a
valuable institution, built and worked on the
separate cottage principle, no communication
existing between the houses but by the subway
running from end to end, by which each block is
supplied direct from the kitchen.   The Church
forms the centre block, and is a striking feature
in the plan.   The Hospital stands in a most
beautiful situation about a mile to the west of

Ventnor, on the St. Lawrence Road, perfectly protected from all northerly winds by the range of Downs in the rear. Each house faces due south, and has double verandahs over-looking pleasure grounds of six acres in extent. "The Queen is Patron, and has been a liberal contributor to the funds of the charity. The institution has frequently been visited by Royalty. In 1888 Her Majesty made a special visit of inspection, travelling for the first time by the I.W. Railway. In several cases a house has been built and fitted throughout at the sole expense of one person, and these houses have been named after their charitable donors.

The Sea-side Home of the London City Mission is located at the foot of St. Boniface Down—the building having been presented to the Society by Mrs Huish, of Combewood, Bonchurch. To this establishment all the Missionaries in connection with the Society—about 500—are sent each summer for two or three weeks, to recoup after arduous City exertions. Those who are delicate, and require a mild climate in winter, are sent here for a change.

St. Catherine's Home for patients in advanced consumption is in Grove-road, and is under the charge of nursing sisters from St. Margaret's, East Grinstead.

The Convalescent Home of the Royal Hants Hospital is situated in Madeira Road.

Ministers' Home and Rest, 1, South View, Madeira Road.

Ventnor and Bonchurch Literary and Scientific Institution was established in the year 1847 and is situated in the High-street. The well-known Rev. James White, of Bonchurch, was the first president. Here are two interesting and local relics of the old French war, both of which were washed out of the chalk cliff, and found on Ventnor Beach. One is an 18-pounder cannon-ball, which by breaking in half has disclosed a perfect seven-pound ball inside it. The other is a specimen of chain-shot, and has a seven-pound ball at each end. The length is about fourteen inches. It is pecfect and fine. Both were presented by old Mr. Hall, who was in the Coastguard and a geologist. Here also will be found nine shelves of fossils and shells, besides three fine fragments of a Samian vessel which Mr. Norman a geologist, believed to have been found at Bonchurch. The Library now contains a large number of books. Many improvements have been carried out by the munificence of the President, the Right Hon. Sir Lawrence Peel, Bart.

The Castle Club, is open to residents and visitors. There is a reading room well supplied with newspapers, etc. There are also smoking and billiard rooms.

Freemasonry is to the fore in Ventnor. The warrant of the Yarborough Lodges, dates from the year 1848, when the Earl of Yarborough was D.G.M. of England, and it was continued down to the year 1869, when from various circumstances, the working of the Lodge was discontinued. In November 1876, a resuscitation was determined upon, and is now successfully worked in a Masonic Hall, adjoining Spary's Posting Establishment in the High-street.

There are extensive Recreation Grounds in Steephill Road, tastefully laid out.

Steephill—a splendid Castellated Mansion, in modern Gothic—is a prominent object. It was built by Mr. Hambrough, 1830-31. It was occupied for some time by the Empress of Austria, who heartily joined in the Steeplechases of the neighbourhood. The Gothic Tower is a great landmark. The main beauty of the Castle is its extensive, charming and diversified grounds. Being a modern town, there is not much to interest the antiquarian. Here are fig and orange trees, exotic plants, etc., blooming in the open, in abundance. It has been erroneously supposed that the climate is unpleasantly hot, which is not a fact.

A favourite place of resort is the Western

Esplanade.   Its extension eastward as far as Collin's Point portrays the natural beauties of the place to the visitors.

The Pier is constructed of wrought iron girders of the "Warren" type, carried on cast iron columns.   The total length is 645ft. and 23ft. wide.   The head of the Pier is raised 2ft. above the other portion.   It is 125ft. long, and 92ft wide, and affords ample accommodation for promenaders.   Here Bands play selections of music throughout the Season.   From the head of the Pier there is a fine view of the Town, Cliffs, and Downs at the back of the Town. There is an excellent Landing Stage.

To the North of Ventnor are the towering and beautiful DOWNS.

St. Boniface Down was thus spoken of by Mr. Edward Miall :—" A giant sentinel, who keeps watch over the snugly-ensconced town at its foot, and shields it, summer and winter, from the north wind.   The ascent is steep enough to test the soundness of your lungs, but the distance to the summit is not so great as to draw exhaustively upon your strength.   The distance is soon and easily conquered but the triumph is an evanescent one.   Miles of the easiest, breeziest, springiest, blithest walking are now before you (if you can walk and like it), in an atmosphere the purity of which may be felt, over turf which

gives a bounding motion to your steps, with acres
of purple heather scenting the air, and wild
flowers of every hue variegating the ground, and
fluttering moths and butterflies gorgeously
arrayed, and twittering birds skipping to and fro
among the furze, and now and then a hawk poised
over head, and cattle chewing the cud upon the
highest spot within their reach, and an endless
change of sights and sounds suggestive of God's
superabounding goodness. Then, what peeps of
splendid scenery you get, now on this side of the
Island now on that, as with freshened spirits you
almost dance along, and always with the blue sea
as a conspicuous feature of it. "Here you may
drink in health as you drink in pleasure." The
stories of this part of the Island are numerous.
One relates that a certain Bishop, whilst riding
over the Down, lost his way in a thick mist, and
to his horror found himself at the brink of the
precipitous face of the hill ; not knowing what to
do, he threw the reins on the horse's neck, which
at once began to descend the steep slope. His
rider gave himself up for loss, and invoking the
aid of St. Boniface, vowed that· if he reached the
bottom in safety he would give an acre of ground
to the Church which bore his name. Either
through the aid of the saint, or through the sure
footedness of the steed, the bishop safely reached
the bottom of the hill—and the "Bishop's
Acre" now memoralises the descent. It is a
plot of ground at the foot of the Down belonging
to the Rector of Bonchurch.

The Parish Church of St. Catharine, in Church Street, was built in 1836-7, from the designs of Mr. Ebbels, at the cost of Mr. J. Hambrough, who also presented the Parsonage and the original National Schools. A chancel was added in 1840. On the wall of the north aisle is a tablet in memory of Mr. G. A. Martin, M.A., who died at Belgrave House on January 7th, 1867. Dr. Martin was the author of "The History of the Undercliff, its Climate, etc," and his name is otherwise connected with that of Ventnor. Holy Trinity is situated in the vicinity of the eastern entrance to the town. Three sisters are said to have provided the funds for the edifice, the foundation stone of which was laid in 1860, from designs of Mr. Giles, of Taunton, Somersetshire. The spire is 100ft. high. It belongs to the Early Decorated style—and, although not in keeping with classical ideality, yet there is much to admire, notwithstanding the questionable position of the transept, and the heaviness of the aisle windows, etc. The character of the decorations is in good taste, and the nave and side aisles are divided by a light arcade—the clere-story shedding a religious light o'erhead. There are transeptal chapels north and south. The font is of veined alabaster. The stone puplit bears an alto-relievo of the Messiah's Benediction. The reredos, i.e., ornamented screen at the back of the altar, is superbly carved and inlaid. Some fine specimens of carving are observable in the capitals and corbels. The east window of five lights is filled with stained glass—the subject being the *Credo*.

St. Margaret's Mission Church, lower road was erected in 1882.

The population in 1871 numbered 4,841. The Census for 1881 was 5,684. Increase in ten years: 843.

Walks from Ventnor.

To Shanklin, three-and-a-half miles. Up the steps from the Esplanade. The walk embraces views of the coast in the direction of St. Lawrence, Bonchurch, and high down of St. Boniface, Horseshoe Bay, Culver Cliffs, and Foreland Point. The East End Landslip will be especially admired as a quiet retreat of natural beauty and repose. Leaving the thicket the vale of Luccombe is reached, and by path the road from Ventnor to Shanklin, the return journey can be made, or, if preferred, along the shore.

To Shanklin by the shore, past Mill Bay, is a pretty walk. High Post Cliffs rise about 100ft. from the shore, and may be ascended by a winding path to a footway, by which the heavy walking on the shore may be avoided. The view of cliffs, Downs, and sea is grand. Rounding the Yellow Ledge and Horse Ledge Points, Shanklin is approached, and an excellent view

of Sandown Bay, Culver Cliffs, and the fort and
monument on Bembridge Down is obtained.

To St. Boniface Down.—This is a walk which
no tourist should miss, being a very high point
in the Island. One route is from Trinity Church
by the path leading past the Wishing Well;
another up a greensward to Ramskin Bottom;
or perhaps, the best is from the railway station
up the ridge to the Little Town Down, past the
reservoir. The view includes the Needles.

Pleasant excursions may be made by coach to
Blackgang, Alum Bay, Freshwater, Brixton and
other places.

The services at the various places of worship
are at the usual times.

ST. LAWRENCE.

ABOUT two miles from Ventnor is St.
Lawrence. It is situated in a lovely
dingle—one of the most charming spots of the
Undercliff. It is not far from the ruins of
Woolverton. On the summit of the "shute" or
hill, is an ivy-clad Early English Church—
originally the smallest Church in the Kingdom.
Its measurement is only twenty-five feet four-
and-three-quarter inches long, eleven feet one-
quarter inch broad, eleven feet four-and-a-half

inches high. It was formerly twenty feet long, eleven feet broad, six feet high. The first Earl of Yarborough enlarged it somewhat by slightly adding to its length—with a porch and bell-turret. He brought his own dinner bell from Appuldurcombe to call the parishioners to prayer. A new church, built of stone, at a cost of £4,000, from designs by the late Sir Gilbert Scott, was consecrated for service on August 6th, 1878. This building has seating accommodation for 300 persons.

The " crystal well," located near St. Lawrence Church, is noteworthy. It is connected with a curious legend of the locality, respecting the mischievous Hermit of the Culver, through whose influence it is said a pilgrim, in a grey cowl, who had visited the Holy Land, was assassinated—thus fulfilling the prophecy :—

> When sainted blood in the burn shall well,
> It shall light a flame so hot and snell,
> Shall fire the burg from lock to fell,
> Nor sheeting bide its place to tell,
> And Culvert's Nass shall ring its knell.

According to the legend, the prophecy was culminated by the burning of a town, which, it is said, stood on the site now occupied by Woolverton Wood.

APPULDURCOMBE,

OR the Valley of Apple Trees, is a mansion, and displays much magnificence and classical taste. It was begun in 1710 by Sir

Robert Worsley, and finished by his successor, Sir Richard Worsley.   The soil is very rich, and affords excellent pasturage ; beeches of uncommon magnitude, interspersed with venerable oaks, from the back-ground above the house ; the different eminences command most extensive and grand prospects, being 400 feet above the sea.   On the east is seen St. Helens roads, Spithead and Portsmouth ; on the west the cliffs of Freshwater, the Dorsetshire coast, and the Isle of Portland ; on the north is a view of the New Forest and the Solent, on the south is the British Channel.

On the summit of the park is an obelisk of Cornish granite, nearly seventy feet in height, erected to the memory of Sir Richard Worsley. At Appuldurcombe there was formerly a cell of Benedictine Monks.   It was made subordinate to the Abbey of St. Mary de Montsburg, in Normandy, by Richard de Redvers, founder of that Abbey.   It was the seat of the late Lord Yarborough, now a college where gentlemen are prepared for all examinations, and Colonial life, by the principal, Mr. A. Morse.   Wroxall station on the Isle of Wight Railway is close by.

NEWCHURCH, ASHEY DOWN, and ARRETON.

NEWCHURCH Parish was formerly the largest (Brading excepted) in the Island, it crossed the whole Island, and included the towns of Ryde and Ventnor. Both these towns were, however, in 1867, made separate from Newchurch.

The Church of All Saints stands on a rising ground, and commands extensive views. The register dates from the year 1676.

ASHEY DOWN affords a good view from its summit, where there is a triangular pyramid about twenty feet high; this pyramid serves as a beacon to guide ships sailing into St. Helens or Spithead. It is described by the Rev. Leigh Richmond in his " Annals of the Poor." At Ashey, Agnes Porter, a widow, was burnt at the stake for witchcraft, in the reign of Elizabeth. The Down is 424 feet above the sea. The summit of the Down affords THE finest view in the Island. Newchurch Church, on one hill, is a prominent object, and there are several patches of farms, houses, etc. Turning towards the east there is the boundless ocean.

ARRETON. The pretty village of Arreton is about three miles from Newport, over the Down, lying at its foot. This is a fertile part of the " Beautiful Isle." Here is an old Church dedicated to St. George, with some quaint epitaphs in the churchyard, and the village possesses considerable interest from its being the

G

birth-place of Elizabeth Wallbridge, the " Dairyman's Daughter," immortalized by the pen of
Leigh Richmond in the following lines :—

> "Stranger ! if e'er by chance or feeling led
> Upon this hallowed turf thy footsteps tread,
> Turn from the contemplation of the sod,
> And think on her whose spirit rests with God.
> Lowly her lot on earth—but He, who bore
> Tidings of peace and blessings to the poor,
> Gave her His truth and faithfulness to prove,
> The choicest treasures of his boundless love, —
> (Faith that dispell'd affliction's darkest gloom ;
> Hope, that could cheer the passage to the tomb ;
> Peace, that not hell's dark legions could destroy,
> And love, that filled the soul with heavenly joy.)
> Death of its sting disarm'd, she knew no fear,
> But tasted heaven e'en while she lingered here.
> Oh, happy saint ! may we like thee be blest ;
> In life be faithful, and in death find rest !"

[On the north side of the Burial Ground is
her tomb—the epitaph here alluded to possessing
more than ordinary interest.]

Arreton is the largest parish in the Island.

There are two large barrows on the Down, in
which were discovered some Roman armour.

A walk through Merston on to Chale Church
is delightful. The Church was built in the
reign of Henry I., wherein is a monument of
Major-General Sir Henry Worsley, G.C.B. Over
the vestry door are the remains of a mural painting, with the words : " And Jacob awakened out
of his sleep." The churchyard is " bare, bleak
and melancholy," and the sea has left its mark
upon it. Most of the unfortunate persons

wrecked in the " Clarendon," October 11th, 1836, are buried here.

BLACKGANG CHINE.—This spot should not be missed. It can be reached by a road near Chale Church. Blackgang signifies " black-path," and is so called on account of the blackness of its rocks. From the sea the aspect is wildly picturesque and savagely grand. The height is nearly as great as St. Catherine's Hill above (about 770ft.) The view comprises the whole of the coast to the Needles, with the Dorsetshire coast in the distance. Waters rush from the hill, excavating two chasms, which afterwards unite ; the stream then runs faster in a deep 200 yards channel, till it comes to an iron-stone grit rock precipice, over which it falls in a perpendicular cascade to the shore, seventy feet below. It is only after heavy rains that there is much water in the Chine.

WOOTTON.

A VERY small village, situate mid-way between Ryde and Newport. The term Wootton is probably a modification of "Wood-town," the main road being reached by a prettily-wooded copse. A long bridge and causeway carries the main road over the river and is over 800ft. in length. The Parish Church dedicated to St. Edmund is built of Gothic stone with a Norman doorway. Here are

G 2

several marble tablets to the memory of the Shute and White families. It is a small but ancient building. There is also an iron church at Wootton Common. The Creek—sometimes termed Fishhouse Creek—takes its name from the village of that name — runs through a wooded country. Here, formerly a good deal of war-ship and yacht building was done. Near it stood the Old Manor House (now a farm-house, where Henry VII. spent a night in 1499).

King's Quay is a small inlet associated by tradition with the memory of King John, who, it is said dwelt in its retired neighbourhood for three months after the signature of Magna Charta.

NEWPORT.

AN inland town, called the capital of the Island. It is situated in a pleasant Vale on the river Medina, and is a market town.

The Town Hall is partly supported by Ionic columns; the whole building cost £10,000, and was completed in 1816. In 1887-8 a handsome clock tower was erected in commemoration of Her Majesty's Jubilee. In the large room is a statue of Chief Justice Fleming, with a medallion of Guido Fawkes. In the Council chamber is a tablet, on which is inscribed the names of the various mayors from 1607 down to the present time.

Chief Justice Fleming was born in the Isle of

Wight, called to the Bar in 1574 ; Recorder of London 1594 ; Solicitor General, 1595 ; Exchequer Baron, 1604 ; Lord Chief Justice, 1607. The inhabitants of Newport presented the Corporation with a good portrait of their Recorder, the late Leonard Thomas Worsley Holmes, B.A., etc., which now hangs in the Council Chamber.

Newport Free Grammar School, built in the reign of James I., was the building selected by King Charles for his residence during the time occupied by the Treaty of Newport. The King continued here for sixty-one days, and dated his letters—From "Our Court at Newport." The oftquoted Treaty was signed in the room since used as a school-room. Charles was seized in the bedroom he used in this house, in which was supposed to be a secret passage through which the King might escape. In 1858 some workmen discovered the entrance to a secret passage at the top of the house—by which the King would very probably have made his final escape, if the soldiers had not arrested him in his bedroom so quickly.

In the room where the secret passage is located there is a curiously carved mantlepiece. In place of a hearthstone some old Dutch tiles are inserted. These tiles are forty in number, and consist of four rows of ten each. Their designs are all from Scripture, and form a highly interesting and instructive series.

The "Bull Inn," since named the "Bugle Hotel," was occupied by the Commissioners.

The "George Tavern" was the place of assemblage for the Royalists and stood on the south side of High-street, but it has long since been pulled down.

In 1377 the French devastated the town, and they set it on fire again in the reign of Edward IV. In 1582-4 the plague almost decimated the town. Dead carts blocked up the road to Carisbrooke, and the Cemetery was so crowded that a graveyard was formed round Newport Church.

St. Thomas's New Church, erected in conse- quence of the complete decay of the Old Church, is a beautiful building. The funds liberally contributed by townsmen, were largely aug- mented by the Queen and Prince Consort. The Prince laid the stone in August, 1854. The west entrance is most noticeable, near which are grouped several monuments from the old church ; also the font, and a most curiously-carved pulpit. The builders were Messrs. Dashwood of Ryde. The monuments include that of the Princess Elizabeth, which was erected at the sole expense of Queen Victoria (who also had two stained- glass windows erected). The Princess Elizabeth is represented as reclining at full-length on one side, her face resting on the last gift of her

CARISBROOKE CASTLE.

ANCIENT AND WELL PRESERVED HISTORICAL CASTLE,

The Prison of King Charles the 1st and his ill-fated Daughter,
Princess Elizabeth.

father—an open Bible—in which position it is said she died. The Bible is open at the text: "Come unto Me all ye that labour and are heavy laden, and I will give you rest."

The likeness is faithful, being from a portrait in Her Majesty's possession. The monument is of pure Carrara marble, in an ornamental shrine, and is one of Baron Marochetti's best productions. The inscription is as follows: "To the memory of Princess Elizabeth, daughter of Charles I., who died at Carisbrooke Castle on Sunday, September 8th, 1650, and is interred beneath the chancel of this Church. This monument is erected, as a token of respect for her virtues, and of sympathy for her misfortunes, by Victoria R., 1856."

Rumour says the Princess' body was embalmed, and then placed in a leaden coffin, open to the gaze of her attendants for fourteen days, and then brought in a borrowed coach from Carisbrooke Castle, the mayor and aldermen meeting the corpse at the end of the town. The coffin was placed in a small arched vault in the middle of the east part of the chancel and the letters E. S. cut in the adjacent wall. The vault, however, was forgotten in course of time, until 1793, when some workmen, employed in making a new grave for the remains of the Hon. Septimus Harry West, sixth son of the Earl of Delaware, discovered the coffin.

The new window above the monument was given by the young ladies of the congregation, and is known as " The Maiden's Window."

There is also here the curious monument of Sir Edward Horsey, Knight. The effigy is in full armour, and the hands are held up, joined, as if in prayer.

Among the representatives of Newport have been : Lucius Carey, second Viscount Falkland ; William Stephens, Esq. ; Lord Cutts ; Sir Thomas Holmes, Knight ; H. J. Temple, the late Viscount Palmerston ; Sir Arthur Wellesley, the great Duke of Wellington ; Right Hon. George Canning ; Charles Wykenham-Martin, Esq., and Charles Cavendish Clifford, Esq.

In the Carisbrooke road, a public memorial has been erected to the late Sir John Simeon, Bart., who represented the Isle of Wight in Parliament several years. He was the first Roman Catholic who ever sat in the House of Commons.

Newport is connected by rail with the principal towns of the Island. The first line was opened in 1862, and connected Cowes ; the second in 1875, to Ryde direct ; the third from Newport to Sandown the same year ; the fourth to Freshwater and Yarmouth was opened in 1889.

Walks from Newport.

To West Cowes, five miles. The carriage road is past the Grammar School and up Hunny Hill, on to Parkhurst Barracks and Parkhurst Prison. The Barracks were erected in 1798, and provide accommodation for from 2,000 to 3,000 soldiers; the Prison is chiefly used for convicts, and will contain about 1,000. The towers of Osborne House and Whippingham and Northwood Churches are in sight nearly the whole of the way. On arriving near the Horse Shoe Inn, one of the most extensive views on the Island is obtained.

To Shorwell, five miles. Past Carisbrooke, through a secluded vale, and over the chalk Downs. The remains of some ancient Pictish villages will be found at Rowborough and Westcourt Bottoms. Proceeding to the left from Carisbrooke, pass through Clatterford and Plash. Ancient Barrows and burial grounds will be found on the hills. Passing down the hill under a rustic wooden bridge to the well-wooded grounds of Northcourt, Shorwell village is reached.

To Pan Down and St. George's Down, one-and-a-half miles. The views include a fine combination of scenery, presenting the estuary of the Medina, Cowes Harbour, the Solent and the Hampshire coast. The descent may be made to Arreton by a lovely lane. The Princess

Cecilia, third daughter of Edward IV. had her residence on St. George's Down.

The services at the various places of worship in Newport are at 10.30 and 6.30.

GODSHILL.

GODSHILL is about five-and-a-half miles from Newport. It has a fine Church on the top of a very steep hill. According to an old tradition, the foundations were first built at the foot of the hill, but every night the materials were carried to the summit by invisible hands; hence the term "God's hill." The Church, dedicated to All Saints, contains monuments of the Worsley family from the 15th to the 19th century. The building itself is of a spacious cruciform character, with a fine pinnacled tower.

In the Church is an oil painting of " Daniel in the the Lion's Den," which, if not by the veritable Rubens is a splendid specimen of his style. It was presented to the Church by a former Earl of Yarborough. A similar picture was purchased by the Duke of Hamilton for £2,600.

Here are monuments of Sir John Leigh and Mary, his wife, who died in the reign of Henry VIII. There are numerous other tablets, brasses and tombs. It is one of the Churches built by

William Fitz Osborne, directly after the conquest. The register dates from the year 1690.

A new peal of bells was subscribed for in celebration of the Queen's Jubilee.

The Nonconformists are represented by Wesleyan and Baptist Chapels.

CARISBROOKE CASTLE.

THE origin, erection and grand ruins of this Castle demonstrate the changing history of the Island, dating back to the time of the ancient Britons, who built a fortress on the spot.

Carisbrooke Castle is believed to have commanded, or overawed the road used in the tin trade, from Gurnard Bay to Puckaster Cove.

When the Romans possessed the Isle of Wight, invaded and subdued by Vespasian in the reign of the Emperor Claudius, the conquerors enlarged the fortress on account of its position for military purposes.

From this period, (about forty-five years before the Christian era), the records on the subject are sparse, until the year 530 when, according to the wording of a Saxon chronicle, it was besieged, and after some opposition, taken by Cerdic, the first monarch of the kingdom of West Saxons.

Cerdic bestowed it on one of his Generals,
(Whitgaraburg), who gave his name to the fortress after he had strengthened it. The pronunciation and spelling at length became fixed
in the title of Carisbrooke, which assumed a
castelled form in the year 693.

The actual Castle, as now understood, was,
according to Doomsday Book, built by William
Fitz Osborne, Earl of Hereford, soon after the
Conquest of 1066. The walls are fourteen feet
thick, on an artificial mound, from which there
is an interesting view. Keats wrote : " I do not
think I shall ever see a ruin to surpass Carisbrooke Castle." It is densely clad with ivy, and
smooth turf has draped the trench walks. The
Castle is arrived at from Newport by a
picturesque archway entrance, erected in
Elizabeth's reign, and bearing date 1568. A
moat, now filled with wild flowers, etc., is
spanned by a stone bridge, crossing which we
reach the stately gate-house, with its ponderous
cross-barred gates, and grand circular towers
above. Walking to the left one may see the
portion in which King Charles was imprisoned
for many months.

The actual window from which the King
attempted to escape is blocked up, but its exact
locality is easily discernible, it being adjacent to
the only buttress on this side of the Castle.

The king, when hard pressed, had thought it

advisable to absent himself for a time ; being able to cross unrecognised, as he thought, to the Isle of Wight, he fancied that the Castle of Carisbrooke would afford him a splendid hiding place, where he could ascertain the period when a reaction might be taken advantage of by him and his adherents. He felt assured that the Governor of Wight, Colonel Hammond, was a Royalist and would assist him ; but the Governor was in the service of the Cromwell party. Charles would, however, have escaped at the first attempt if he had taken the precaution to ascertain if the bars of his department would permit him to get through. Everything else had been admirably arranged. Success was certain if he could have placed himself outside his chamber ; but he could not force his body through the bars. It was with great difficulty he extricated himself from his awkward position and signalled to his friends, by placing a lamp in his window, that he had failed. In the second attempt he had cut asunder the bars of his window by aquafortis and a saw ; but when he was about to descend from the window the Governor and his men arrived. Escape was then hopeless. He therefore, closed the casement and returned to his bed. On the 29th November, 1649, he was seized by the army at Newport, and conveyed to Hurst Castle, on the coast of Hampshire. On his way thither, meeting Mr. Edward Worsley, from whom he had received considerable attention, and who had been very active in attempting his escape, the Monarch gave him the watch out of his pocket, as a token of remembrance. The watch is still preserved in the family; it is of silver, large and clumsy in its form. The case is neatly ornamented with filigree; but the movements are of very ordinary workmanship, and wound up with catgut. From Hurst Castle he was taken to Westminster Hall, tried and committed; sentence of death having been pronounced upon him. On the 30th January 1649, he was executed on the scaffold in front of the banqueting house Whitehall, by a masked executioner. He was born at Dumfermline, Scotland in the year 1600, possessed a fine genius, and was a powerful writer. On the "death" of the King, his children—Henry, Duke of Gloucester, and the Princess Elizabeth —were conveyed to the Castle, in August, 1650; the Princess who was at the age of 15, to have been apprenticed, by the authorities, to a button-maker, died in the following month—the Duke remaining three years, when he went to Holland.

The ancient " Place of Arms," was converted into the present tilt-yard, or bowling green, for the amusement of Charles I. Here in the days of yore, the gay tournament was held, and each gallant Knight encountered his mailed antagonist. The unsightly mansion has been made out of the original hall; formerly a strong wall connected it with the Keep. One of two chapels within the

Castle precincts has been brought to light.
Adjacent to the Chapel, southward, there stood
originally, the principal apartment of the
Castle ; there is here a fine ancient staircase.
There are covered ceilings of the "Georgian
era" in some of the Governor's rooms.

The massive old Keep still exists on an
artificial mound, commanding a view of the rest
of the castle, and of miles of charming scenery
around. Some effort is necessary to reach the
Keep, there being a flight of seventy-four steps,
none too easy to ascend. Within the Keep is a
smaller flight of steps, leading to an irregular
polygon, fifty feet broad, formed by the walls of
the old tower. The "Donjon Well," of repu-
tedly fabulous depth, has long been filled up.
There is, however, another well here, which is
an object of attraction. It is near the entrance,
nearly 200 feet deep, including about three
dozen feet of water. On one side of the well-
house room is an enormous box-wheel. This
wheel is supposed to be unique, and to resemble
the one not far from the "Devil's Dyke," near
Brighton. The treadwheel is worked by a
donkey, "Jacob," who enters the contrivance
and walks (without advancing) till a bucket of
water is drawn up. Jacob, like his predecessors,
is a general favourite, and performs his work
"in a quiet sort of way," most amusing to
tourists. A predecessor of Jacob is related to
have performed his work for a period of forty

years, and then was pensioned off to the paddock, there to enjoy his old age " in clover." A glass of water is thrown down the well, and the visitor notes the time which elapses before water to water comes. Then a small lamp is lowered by a windlass ; and it is interesting to note the circle of light tapering till the lamp floats below at a dizzy depth. The fall of a pin makes a strange reverberation for so slender an object.

The dungeon at Carisbrooke Castle seems to have been used in modern times, for it is mentioned in a petition against Lord Culpeper (Captain of the Island) assuming to himself the title of Governor, that he exercised an arbitrary power in the said Island, sometimes proceeding so far, as, by his sole arbitrary power, to imprison persons in the noisome dungeon in Carisbrooke Castle.

Jerome, Earl of Portland, who succeeded his father in 1634 was Captain of the Isle of Wight, and rendered obnoxious to the Parliament, by his attachment to the royal cause. During his absence orders were despatched to Moses Read, Mayor of Newport, to seize the Castle and its occupiers, consisting of the Countess of Portland, Colonel Brett, and a garrison of twenty men. The Mayor, at the head of four hundred sailors, and the Newport Militia, marched to attack the Castle. The noble-minded Countess resolved not to surrender the citadel except on honourable terms, and both by precept and example, this heroic lady animated her little band. With a lighted match she proceeded resolutely to one of the castions, and declared she would discharge the first cannon against the besiegers. The gallant conduct of the Countess and her band of heroes, induced the Mayor to offer favourable terms of capitulation, to which the Countess acceded.

The Castle and grounds occupy about twenty acres. The exterior forms a delightful prom- enade of upwards of a mile, commanding charm- ing and extensive views of the surrounding country. The Castle is 300ft. above the level of the valley.

The old Roman road may still be traced, and a large Roman Villa, adjacent to the Parsonage, was discovered in 1859.

Carisbrooke Church is one of the finest and one of the oldest in the Island. It was built in 1064. In 1071 it was richly revived by William Fitz Osborne. The Church is dedicated to St. Mary, and is supposed to stand upon the ground of a Saxon Church, built some hundreds of years before the Norman Conquest. This first church is supposed to have been called " The Church of the Fair Valley." Saxon implements have been discovered in the vicinity. The present church of Carisbrooke has eight splendid toned bells and are " perhaps as musical as ever were cast."   The tower is a fine specimen of the solid architecture of our fore-fathers. The pulpit bears date 1685.   The chancel and north aisle were demolished in the reign of Elizabeth.   A singular monument to Lady Wadham, with six niches in the background, is worthy of notice.

In Carisbrooke churchyard, under date 1747, appears the following epitaph :—

> Here lyes a man the farmers loved,
> Who always to them faithful proved,
> And dealt with freedom justly fair,
> An honest miller, all declare.

On the tomb of Charles Dixon, a blacksmith, is the following :—

> My sledge and hammer lie reclined,
> My bellows pipes have lost their wind,
> My fire's extinct, my forge decay'd,
> My vice is in the dust now laid ;
> My coal is spent, my iron's gone,
> My nails are drove, my work is done,
> My fire-dried corpse here lies at rest,
> My soul, smoke-like, soars to be blest.

On another tombstone is the following :—

Here lieth the body of the Right Worthy William Keeling. Groom of the Chamber to our Sovereign Lord King James ; General for the Hon. East India Adventures, whither he was thrice by them employed ; and dying in this Isle at the age of 42, An. 1619, Sept. 19th, hath this remembrance here fixed by his loving and sorrowful wife, Ann Keeling :

> Fortie and two years in this vessel fraile,
> On the rough seas of life did KEELING saile,
> A merchant fortunate, a captain bould,
> A courtier gracious, yet, alas ! not old.
> Such wealth, experience, honour, and high praise,
> Few winne in twice so many years or days ;

TOTLAND BAY.

Rising high class Watering Place with magnificent Bay of firm White Sand,
and immediately adjoining Alum Bay and the Needles.

For what the world admired, he deëm'd but drosse,
For Christ—without Christ all is gain but losse,
For Him and for His love, with meere cheere,
To the Holy Land his last course he did steere:
Faith served for sails, Sacred Word for yard,
    Hope was his anchor, glorie his reward ;
    And thus with gales of grace, by happy ventir,
Through straits of death, heav'n's harbour he did enter.

EAST and WEST COWES.

LELAND says : " There be two new castles set up and furnished at the mouth of Newport, that is the only haven in the Isle of Wight to be spoken of. That, that is set up on the east side of the haven is called EAST COW and that, that is set up on the west side is called the WEST COW, and is the bigger of the two." Cowes Harbour is an estuary formed by the junction of the river Medina with the Solent. The custom-house for the whole Island is here, and in consequence much business is transacted at this port. The population in 1881, was 2543.

East Cowes Castle was erected by Henry VIII. from the ruins of a religious house but has now vanished, the sight being known as " Old Castle Point."

The first stone of St. James's Church was laid by the Queen, when she was Princess Victoria, on September 6th, 1831.

East Cowes Park comprises 160 acres. Viscount Gort has given a Recreation Ground for the public.

WEST COWES. Yachts are generally seen on the broad estuary of the Medina, and some of the best yachts that ever sailed are from the Cowes Yard. The yachting season is from May 1st to November 1st. West Cowes Castle was formerly one of the circular forts built by Henry VIII., but as a fortress it became almost value-less after the erection of the massive forts at Yarmouth and Hurst, and the Government sold it to the Royal Yacht Squadron Club. It is now used as a Club House. The Esplanade and Beach, with pretty residences behind, their lawns sloping to the sea will be noticed. St. Mary's Church is very handsome, it is built of Swansea rubble and Bath stone. The carved reredos was presented by Mr. Pascall Atkey, and the splendid organ by Miss Ward and Mrs. Beckford. The cost of the edifice was £6,000. It contains 960 sittings. Holy Trinity Church is built of brick, and is Gothic in style. It contains 700 sittings. The cost of the building was £6,897 and was the gift of Mrs. S. Goodwin. The Recreation Ground covers nine acres, and was presented to the town by Mr. G. W. Ward, in 1869.

Prince's Green is an excellent promenade. It was given by Mr. George Robert Stephenson, in 1864, is near the sea, and extends one thousand feet. The Docks and Ship Builders' Yards

COWES, (ON THE SOLENT,)

Favorite Sea-side Resort during the Yachting Season.
Excellent Bathing and Boating.

deserve special notice. There is a brass and iron foundry ; manufactory for wire rope ; extensive sail-making ; oyster fisheries, etc.

The Royal London Yacht Club have a branch here, and in the season Cowes is exceedingly lively.

The Hampshire coast, New Forest, Calshot Castle and Southampton Water are clearly seen. Henry VIII. landed here, also James I., Charles I., and James II., when Duke of York.

OSBORNE.

OSBORNE HOUSE, the residence of Her Majesty, was built by a Mr. Blachford, who married Mr. Mann's grand-daughter and heiress. Their descendant, Lady Isabella Blachford, sold the estate to Her Majesty in 1840. The Queen purchased, as opportunities arose, till the estate now comprises 5,000 acres. Her Majesty also had the house razed, and the present mansion erected, the late Prince Consort it is said assisting in the preparation of the designs. The new palace, which was built by Mr. E. Cubitt, in the Palladian style of architecture, on the basis of the principles of the celebrated Italian architect, Palladio, who built the Olimpico at Vicenza. The bell-tower is ninety feet high, and the flag-tower 107 feet. The Queen occupies the apartments in advance of the latter.

The rooms are crowded with objects of taste and *vertu*, sculptures by our most eminent artists, rare specimens of modern painters, and all the refinements which a cultivated taste could suggest. The gardens are arranged in terraces, the lawn sloping to the water's edge, where there is a small private jetty. There are most delightful views therefrom, a combination of almost everything beautiful in scenery. Here is the Prince's Model Farm, with spacious kennels for hounds, and excellent labourers' cottages, with the Albert and Victoria Almshouses erected by the Queen. Visitors cannot obtain admission to either house or grounds. On the East Cowes Road the lodges will be observed, and their fanciful design will attract attention.

———

WHIPPINGHAM CHURCH which was erected at the cost of the Queen and the late Prince Consort, is a pretty edifice. The Queen is a worshipper there when staying at Osborne. There are grand stained windows and admirably tasteful decorations. The main feature is a marble monument (by Theed) to the Prince Consort. Inscription : " To the beloved memory of Francis Albert Charles Emmanuel, Prince Consort, who departed this life December 14th, 1861, in his 43rd year. This monument is placed in the Church, erected under his directions, by his broken-hearted and devoted widow, Queen Victoria, 1864." Princess Beatrice and

Prince Henry of Battenberg were married in this Church.

NORRIS CASTLE the residence and property of the Duke of Bedford is thickly clad with ivy, and commands a most splendid prospect. Opposite is the broad Southampton water. The Castle was built for Lord Henry Seymour. George IV. was entertained here in 1819, and the Queen (when Princess Victoria), resided here, with the Duchess of Kent, in 1831. The Crown Prince and Princess of Germany recently stayed here.

NEWTOWN, in Calbourne parish, between Cowes and Freshwater, was at one time a flourishing market town ; but now it reminds one of some lines in Goldsmith's " Deserted Village." The legend of its having once been the town of Francheville, invested with myriads of rats, which were piped to the river and drowned by the " Pied Piper," who, being refused his promised reward, also piped away the young folks —so that when the French came in 1377 they met no opposition—is reminissive of a similar story told of the town of Hamel, Brunswick— where the rats were drowned in the Weser and the children piped into a hole in the hill side that closed after them.

SWAINSTONE.—This delightful residence is the seat of Sir Barrington Simeon, Bart. It is situated in a fertile valley, luxuriantly wooded and commands fine views of the Solent ; it is erected on the site of an ancient palace of the Bishops of Winchester.

YARMOUTH.

THIS little town belongs to the past so far as its "glory" goes. It is situate at the mouth of the western Yar. It is crossed by a long bridge connecting the town with the promontory of Freshwater, the residence of the Poet Laureate. It was burnt by the French in 1337 and again in 1544. After the latter event Henry VIII. erected Yarmouth Castle.

From the George Hotel steps, Charles I. delivered an address to the inhabitants, on the way to his imprisonment in Carisbrooke Castle.

The Church of St. James' is a plain structure erected in 1611 ; in the south chapel is the finest piece of sculpture in the Island—a monument consisting of the life-size statue of Sir Robert Holmes, Governor of the Isle of Wight from 1667 to 1692. A long Latin inscription records his deeds.

In the early part of the year 1881 four magnificent stained glass windows were placed in Yarmouth Parish Church. They are splendid works of art, and approximate in tint to the ancient coloured windows, being admirably executed by Messrs. Powell and Sons, Whitefriars, London. Two of these windows were given by Mrs. Squires, in memory of members of her family who were for so many years such respected inhabitants. Mrs. Hodges, a daughter of Mrs. Squires, presented the third window, in memory of her husband. The fourth window was given by the parish in remembrance of the Rev. J. D. Ostreham, who, for a short time during the last restoration of the Church held the rectory of the parish.

In 1871 the population of Yarmouth was 806 ; the population in 1881, according to the census, was 799, showing a decrease of twenty-seven. Those, however, who desire longevity might do worse than live in Yarmouth. The return of 1881 census included two men each eighty years old, and two ladies, one at ninety-one and the other ninety-nine.

Single Tours.

From Ryde to Newport, Shorwell, (interesting Church with stone pulpit, and iron frame that used to contain an hour glass ; remains of mural paintings,) to Brixton (Brighstone), a delightful village on a sunny table-land. Back by Gat-combe formerly the seat of the Worseley family, is situate in a most beautiful valley. It is three-and-a-half miles south-west from Newport.

The Church of St. Olave is a very ancient structure. In the church is a cross-legged oaken effigy of a knight in complete armour, lying on the right side, and his feet supported by a curiously carved animal : at the head a cherub with out-spread wings.

The Register dates 1560. Thence to Arreton.

From Ryde, through Arreton, Godshill and Chale to Blackgang. Back through Niton, a very pretty village having many handsome houses. The Church of St. John is built of free-stone in the transitional style, it is very ancient and was the gift of William Fitz Osborne to his Abbey in Normandy. Charles I. gave it to Queen's College, Oxford.

ST. CATHERINE'S LIGHT-HOUSE.— The visitor should not fail to see St. Catherine's light-house, which is said to contain the most powerful electric light in the world, designed by Sir James Douglas, Engineer-in-chief to the Trinity House.

A beacon station was erected on St. Catherine's in the fourteenth century, when a certain knight built a chantry and provided an endowment for a priest whose special duty it was to keep a bright light burning at night for the benefit of passing vessels.

In 1785 the Trinity Board built a light-house on the same site, but owing to the mists which so frequently enveloped the hill, the light-house was not of much service.

In 1837 the present light-house was built, the ground on which it stands being 81ft. above high water mark. The building rose to 100ft., but in consequence of the fogs which so frequently enveloped the lantern, it was lowered 40ft. On the 25th March, 1840, the powerful lantern was lighted for the first time, being equal to 740 candles. The tower owing to the soil is three inches out of the perpendicular, but no danger is apprehended, as the foundations have been carried to the rock.

A lantern of 740 candles was considered at the time to be wonderful, but just fancy two lights of three million candle power each, the brilliancy of which is so intense that it would be possible to read a newspaper by their flash a dozen miles off. This is the light now to be seen flashing nightly from St. Catherine's. The following is a description of the machinery in the engine house :—Three of Robey's compound engines, each of 36 horse-power, and two De Meriten's magneto-electric machines, working at a speed of 600 revolutions per minute, each capable of producing a light of 3,000,000 candles.

There are three lamps (only one is used at a time) of the Serrin-Berjot type, modified, the carbons are two-and-a-half inches in diameter, and six pointed star-shape in section. The dioptric lantern is a drum containing sixteen panels of vertical lenses ; this rotates and gives a flash of four seconds, followed by twenty-six seconds' darkness.

There is also a fog-horn, and the syren can be started at any moment, the same engines working the dynamos, driving the compressors. The visitor should hear this musical instrument if possible, as well as see the magnificent flashes of light.

The " Chalybeate " spring was discovered in 1808, by a surgeon of Newport, is celebrated for its medicinal properties.

The Alexandrian Pillar is seventy-two feet high, and bears the following inscription :—" In commemoration of the visit of His Imperial Majesty, Alexander I., Emperor of all the Russias, to Great Britain, in the year 1814, and in remembrance of many years' happy residence in his dominions, this pillar was erected by Michael Hoy."

Through Whitwell, Godshill, Sandown and Brading.

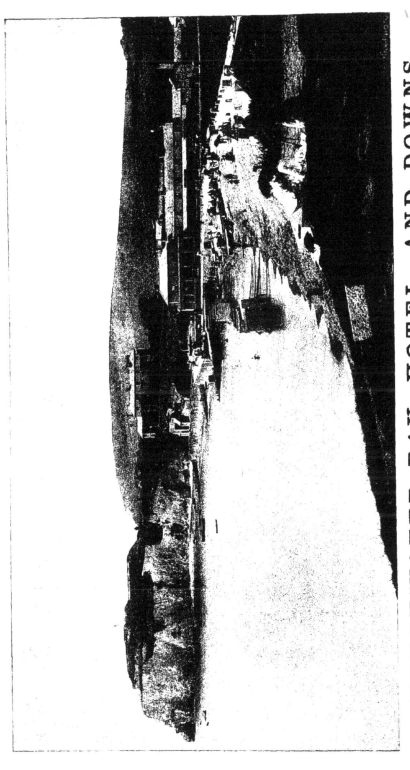

FRESHWATER BAY, HOTEL, AND DOWNS.

Beautiful Landscape Scenery and Rising Watering Place.

From Ryde to Newport and Carisbrooke Castle: to Arreton, Knighton and Ashey Down, and *via* Aldermoor and Smallbrooke, to Ryde.

Three Day's Continued Tour.

FIRST DAY.—From Ryde to Brading, Sandown Bay and Fort, Shanklin Chine, Luccombe Chine, Bonchurch, Ventnor, Steephill Castle, and St. Lawrence,—Thence to Sandrock Hotel, Niton.

SECOND DAY.—To Blackgang Chine, Chale Church, Brighstone. Thence to Brooke, situated between hills, near the sea. Brooke House, the residence of Charles Seeley, Esq., is a noble erection. Here, in 1864, Mr. Seeley, father of the present owner, entertained Garibaldi.—At the base of Brooke Point there is a dangerous reef of Wealdon sandstone rocks, extending a considerable distance into the Sea—half a mile or more; the clays, etc., have been washed away, leaving the rocky ledges. Beyond is a petrified forest, abounding in bones of reptiles, etc. The trees appear to have been submerged on obtaining maturity, and while fresh and vigorous. Some stems have been traced twenty feet, indicating the height of the trees when living, to have been from forty feet to fifty feet.—Thence to Freshwater Gate, the only deep gap in the range of Cliffs and Downs, stretching from the Needles to Brighstone. Here is a battery, mounting eight 68-pounders. There is lovely

scenery here.   Freshwater Cliffs (chalk) are
400 to 600ft. high, and three miles long.   The
Bay is called Watcombe Bay.   In this locality
is Farringford, the home of Lord Tennyson,
D.C.L., M.A., England's Poet Laureate.—Thence
to the Needles' Lighthouse.   The Cliffs taper
bodily but narrowly, at a point into the sea,
beyond which are the three wedged-shaped
Needle Rocks, rising out of the sea, and washed
white with the waves on the southern side.   The
Needles are "three," but there was formerly
another rock—which sailors called "Lot's Wife,"
120ft. high; it fell in 1764.   The Druids of the
race of Coranied designated this rock, tottering
high over the ocean, the sacred stone of Ur.

There was formerly a Lighthouse on Needles'
Point, at an elevation of 447 feet.   During the
year 1858 the present Lighthouse was erected
on the westernmost point of the Needles, 100ft.
high.

The Needles' cave penetrates 300ft. into the
cliff.   Node's Cliffs in Scratchell's Bay are 617ft.
high, and are remarkably picturesque.   Red
streaks, here and there, run down the Cliffs,
which are of a higher shade, into the placid waters
below, whilst the undulating and many shaded
green lands above add to the attraction.
Thousands of birds locate themselves in the
thousand hedges and hollows.   There are numerous Caves here—among them Frenchman's
Hole, ninety feet deep, where a fugitive French

prisoner concealed himself and was starved to death.

Thence to Alum Bay, which derives its name from the quantity of that mineral found on the shore. Here are high cliffs of brilliantly-coloured vertical strata, of remarkable beauty: "One side of it is a wall of glowing chalk, the other a barrier of rainbows!" The height of the Cliffs (with Headon hill above) is 400ft., and the length about a quarter of a mile.

Thence to Totland Bay. The air of this charming fashionable watering place is peculiarly bracing, it has a splendid sandy beach and good bathing accommodation, about two miles from Alum Bay. The view from the sea as the visitor gazes up at the cliffs is grand. The visitor may spend many days in the neighbourhood seeing the beauties of nature in cliff and cave.

The Church contains 300 sittings. Good parsonage and Schools.

The Roman Catholic Chapel stands on an eminence, and commands fine views of the surrounding scenery. The Totland Bay Hotel is replete with every convenience, elegantly fitted and furnished in the most modern style. The Pier is 400ft. in length. In this district there is a large Pottery, where red-ware is made by hand; open to visitors. Totland is in the centre of the interesting Geological strata, and is much frequented by Geologists.

THIRD DAY.—To Yarmouth on the Yar, opposite Lymington. A new Pier has been constructed near.—Thence. to Calbourne, and Westover.—Thence to Carisbrooke Castle, Newport, Cowes and Ryde.

SHALFLEET CHURCH, four miles east of Yarmouth, has curiously carved porches, date of Register, 1604.

Thorley Church dedicated to St. Swithin was erected in 1871. The old Church is standing and the Register dates from 1614.

MOTTISTONE CHURCH has internal fittings of cedar, obtained from a vessel wrecked on the neighbouring coast.—The main attraction here is the LONG STONE—a huge rude mass of stratified iron sandstone. This long Stone, *i.e.*, Logan stone, was one of the three sacred places of the Druids in the Island. It was said that a child's finger could move it so as to swing from its foundation in the summer-breeze—but if the strongest man had guilt upon his soul the rock would remain firm. Here the Druids of the Cimri sacrificed a white bull, sang a hymn to Hu Gadarn (the Supreme Being) and played on their harps whilst invoking the deity's aid. [The third sacred place was the grove of oaks in the Hexel-ground of Yar, better known in modern times as Brading Haven.]

PORTSMOUTH.

DOCKYARD.

THE visitor should not quit the Island without first having a run over to Portsmouth and see the DOCKYARD, etc. Steamers go direct from Ryde Pier to Portsmouth Harbour, (as well as to Southsea and Portsmouth), at frequent intervals daily. A few yards separate the Harbour pier from the Dockyard. Inside the Dockyard Gates there is a waiting room, where a visitor signs his name, and, if not alone, states the number of his party. As a rule, when about half-a-dozen have assembled here, a policeman starts round the Dockyard with them. There is no fee chargeable; still we believe there is nothing to prevent a gratuity being given. It should be understood that by the policeman-conducted tours, one gets only a very cursory glance at the principal objects of interest. If a visitor know, or can secure an introduction to some official so much the better for him. However, in the ordinary way, much is seen of interest. As is generally known, this is one of our principal naval dockyards, covering upwards of three

I

hundred acres. We believe it is unequalled in size, yet extensions are continually necessitated. The mast-house, or rather houses, for there is a range of them on the left-hand side, are first seen, and the size of the "sticks" astonish not a few. Then come an enormous number of heavy anchors. In the boat-house are a number of large collapsing boats, some exhibited open, some shut up, The rope-house, destroyed by fire in 1776, was not the result of an accident, but the work of one John Aitken, (alias "Jack the Painter,") who was executed on a gibbet erected at the Dockyard gates, and his body was afterwards hung in chains on the Common at Southsea. If the policeman-guide should take the party into the smithy, they may well be delighted. Perhaps the greatest of the attractions here will be the great Nasmyth steam hammer, which can be so regulated as to strike a tremendous iron flattener, or to merely crack a nut ; the numerous steam drills, etc., etc., will prove very interesting. From iron to wood, we return to the saw mills, where the perfection of this branch of machinery is seen performing a variety of sawing, turning and other works. Amongst the other wonderful sights are those to be found in the Metal Mills, CopperFoundry, Tarring-house, &c., the perfection of human machinery, the cream of skilled mechanics are seen at work. Visitors can see either a variety of real torpedoes, or models of them. There are almost always some fine vessels either at the wharf or in some of the basins. The visitor should try to get aboard one of the magnificent Indian troopships, one of the war ships, and one of the Royal yachts. There are several building slips and dry docks, the size of which astonishes many, though they are none too large for some of the huge crafts which have grown there. Pairs of large shears, for putting masts into vessels, excite more than a passing glance from their immense height, capable of lifting a weight of 160 tons. The Royal Naval College, the Dockyard church, the Port Admiral's house, the Library, etc., are among the many objects of interest which the visitor should see, but which are too numerous for us to detail. In the cupola of the church is the bell of the "Royal George."

Visitors are admitted between 10 and 12 a.m. and 1.15 and 3 p.m.

H. M. GUNWHARF

IS reached, after leaving the dockyard, from the other side of the harbour pier. The wharf—fronting the Harbour at the junction of Portsmouth and Portsea—commenced its exitence in 1652, on ground reclaimed from the sea. It occupies a space of fourteen acres, and contains, as implied by its name, guns. Here there are "guns and *guns*"—stocks of the smallest make to stocks of the largest. There are also relics and seizures; there is a gun and its carriage recovered from the wreck of the ill-fated "Royal George," after about fifty-seven years. Then there are guns which did belong to other nations, being specimens of those captured by us. Perhaps the greatest attraction will be found in the large building with a green roof (covered with copper) ; here there is an armoury containing no less than 20,000 stand of arms, for use by our soldiers. Here, there are other trophies, in guns, and armour, etc. Much taste is shown in the skilful display of arms, etc. The armoury was built in 1797. To the south-ward—near the pyramids of cannon-shot and bombshell—may be seen some granite shot lodged in our ships during the unsuccessful attempt in the Dardanelles by Sir John Duckworth.

The wharf is open to visitors daily (excepting on Sundays and Saturday afternoons) — in summer from 9.30 to 12, and 2 to 4 ; in winter there is a curtailment of an hour—till 3.

THE HARBOUR

UNDOUBTEDLY has no equal. There is mostly a very strong current, just at the mouth, but inside the water is calm. As to size, we may say that our entire fleet could find a home here if occasion required it, for there is more than a sufficient expanse of deep water at low tide even, with good anchorage. High lands shelter it all round, so that it is really a kind of huge basin. The docks are on the east side, but fortifications and arsenals surround it. The biggest guns are mounted around. As to size, the mouth, (with Portsmouth on one side and Block House Fort on the other) is about 270 yards only, but Gosport and Portsea are hardly reached ere it has widened to nearly a mile. As to length, it extends as far as Fareham, Porchester, etc., and the circumference is about a dozen miles. To see properly, both the harbour and any vessels, a waterman must be engaged. Three "wooden walls" are open to visitors for a few hours every day. There is Nelson's *Victory;* the Admiral's flag-ship "Duke of Wellington," and the well-known training-ship for boys, the "St. Vincent." The particular spot on which Nelson received the "fatal wound" is marked in brass on the "Victory's" deck, and the cockpit to which he was conveyed to die will also be noticed, and other relics of this great naval hero. The Victory, (Nelson's Barge) was thoroughly over-hauled during 1888, and will last for many years to come, unless any unforeseen accident should happen. If in the visit to the dockyard, persons did not board a Royal yacht or a troop-ship they should do so now. The "Vernon," torpedo-ship, and the "Excellent," gunnery ship, etc., should also be inspected. The railway pier has a branch which runs right into the dockyard, and by this means troops are conveyed direct to the troop-ships, etc.

The Joint Railway Company's first-class paddle steamers run from here to Ryde Pier. The approaches to the harbour are very difficult, excepting to those familiar with the landmarks, situation of buoys, etc., so that in time of war the alteration or removal of these would render the entrance of a hostile fleet impossible. The great extent of mud, though reducing the area, available for anchorage, has its advantages as it prevents a rough sea even in the strongest gale.

SPITHEAD.

THIS designation owes its origin to a sand-bank lying on the west side of Portsmouth Harbour entrance. This bank—after running out into the sea for about two miles to the south-east—ends in a "point" popularly called "spit," the promontory naturally receiving title of STITHEAD. The roadstead beyond it, indicated by buoys. Generally some big war-ships are proudly riding between the Portsmouth side and the Isle of Wight.

SPITHEAD FORTS are situated on the Horse Sand—No-man's Land—Spit Bank—and St. Helen's. Exclusive of the last-named, the three forts cost more than one million pounds of the public money. The estimated cost of the fort on the Horse Sand was £424,694 while the companion fort was to cost £462,500. The estimated cost for the Spit Bank Fort was £169,574, while that for the St. Helens and Puckpool Batteries conjoined was £141,799. The expenditure on the St. Helens Battery to March 31st, 1876, was £110,801. The art of constructing heavy guns has, however, been so developed during the last few years, that the design is compromised and the original scale outgrown. The small casements are impracticable for the huge guns now in vogue. The Forts themselves are massive circular structures, chiefly composed of iron and granite, and faced with heavy armour constructed on the plate-upon-plate system. No-man's Land Fort is pierced to carry twenty-four 38-ton guns on the lower tier; twenty-five 18-ton guns on the upper tier. Horse Sand Fort has a similar arrangement. Spit Bank Fort—just at the entrance to Portsmouth Harbour, nearest to the Mainland—is pierced for nine thirty-eight-ton guns, and pierced at the rear for some smaller guns. St Helen's Fort has a small battery, there being casements for two eighteen-ton guns. During 1889 the old guns were removed and were replaced by modern forty-seven-tonners.

Wells have been sunken under the sea, within the forts, at great cost of labour and ingenuity; from which the garrison can in time of war draw their supply of fresh water.

GOSPORT

IS situated on the east side of the harbour, and is worth a cursory visit, at all events. It can be reached from Portsmouth by a floating bridge or steam launch, or from Portsea by launches, which run every five minutes—fare half-penny. There are complete fortifications here, and barracks accommodating 1,000 men, besides providing quarters for officers, and rooms for soldiers' wives. They were completed in 1859. The Royal Clarence Victualling Yard (from which the Queen mostly starts for Osborne) should be seen. Here there are most extensive stores, bakehouses, brewery, cooperage, etc.—Haslar Hospital (for seamen and marines) is situated about a mile to the south of Gosport; a museum here is open to the public. The hospital is 1,600 feet long, and was built for 2,000 patients, but 2,400 have been treated here at one time. A Chapel, etc., is connected with it.—Monkton Fort (modern) a mile off, mounts forty-two heavy guns. There are other forts and batteries which the visitor may like to see. —Holy Trinity Church was built in 1694. The architecture belongs to the Dutch type. It has a beautiful interior, and boasts of an organ erected under the supervision of Handel.

PORTSEA,

IN the neighbourhood of the Dockyard, is a town in itself, attracted no doubt by the yard. It had no existence in 1700, but increased in size very rapidly during the American War. The principal throughfare is Queen Street—so called after Queen Anne. Walking up this, persons may proceed to either Portsmouth, Landport or Southsea. A very large military hospital and the Anglesey Barracks are at Portsea.

PORTSMOUTH TOWN.

PORTSMOUTH Borough includes Portsea, Landport, Southsea, and Kingston. The whole are in what is called Portsea Island. Portsmouth sends two members to Parliament. It is about seventy-two miles S.W. of London, and has a population of 125,102. A fine new Town Hall has been erected, the large room seating over 2,000 persons. The main thoroughfare is High Street, where there is a large Soldiers' Institute, with lecture hall, reading-room, library, billiard-room, etc., for army and navy men. For this all honour and thanks are due to Miss Robinson, "The Soldier's Friend." In this street also are: the Governor's House, Post Office, Guildhall (small) and Market Place. "No. ten" (nearly opposite the Unitarian Chapel) is the house in which the Duke of Buckingham was fatally stabbed by Felton. A square building near, was once the residence of the Governor. The Garrison Chapel used to be adjacent to it, but it has been demolised. In a nitch may be seen a bust of Charles I., encircled by a laurel and oaken wreath ; this was erected by the inhabitants about about 1623.   The body of John Pound, founder of Ragged Schools, lies in the graveyard adjacent the Unitarian Chapel. The large building at the north end of the street, is the Cambridge barracks ; they are very large —extending far back, and having a large yard in the centre.   The Royal Artillery Barracks are in Broad Street.

ROYAL GARRISON CHURCH stands on the site of an old Religious House at the north-west corner of Governor's Green. In 1212 the Bishop of Winchester—Peter de Rupibus— founded and endowed a building which he had caused to be erected as a Hospital for twelve poor men.

This Hospital was, in course of years known as the *Domus Dei*—" House of God,"—and gradually became more and more a distinctly Religious House. During the reign of Henry VIII., at the Dissolution of Monasteries, the endowment was taken away and the place— having been confiscated—was changed into a Governor's Residence.

Until a few years ago, the building was used as an armoury, and was falling into decay, but Government having granted £2000—£3,000 besides having been obtained—the fabric was beautifully restored, Mr G. E. Street, R.A., super-intending the restoration, retaining all ancient reminiscences.

It is now termed " England's Military Cathedral." Herein are stained windows, tattered colours, and many other reminders of past fights and heroes. The tablets on the walls form objects of interest to visitors. Here may be said to be a " Monumental History of England.

The east windows are in memory of Field Marshals. The Lord Raglan, G.C.B. (centre), General Sir C. Napier, G.C.B. (north), and Field Marshal the Lord Clyde, G.C.B. (south). Amongst the tombs in the chapel-yard, is one to the memory of the late Sir Charles Napier, the great Indian General. The tomb is composed of blue granite—the representation being similar to the knights of old. The most noteworthy battles in which he fought are recorded.

ST. THOMAS'S CHURCH, originally built in 1220, and dedicated to St. Thomas-a-Beckett—was partly rebuilt in 1693. The ornamental Saracenic style of the pilasters and clustered pillars may here be compared with the plain Tuscan style of the modern nave. The fine painted window over the Communion Table and the two lateral ones, and the armorial bearings of the donor, the Rev. C. B. Henville, are worth a visit.

Eight fine-toned bells are contained in a latticed erection over the tower. In the lanthorn is a small bell, anciently used to give alarm in case of fire. Crowning the whole, on the top of the building, is a gilt model of a ship six feet ten inches long; length of hull, three feet five inches; from keel to top of mainmast, four feet two inches. On the foremast a small flag is so placed that it moves with the slightest motion of the breeze, indicating in what quarter the wind veers—when not sufficient to move the hull of the ship. This weather-vane weighs eighty-four pounds.

Amongst the many monuments is one erected to the Duke of Buckingham—a favourite of Charles the First—who incurred the displeasure of a former lieutenant, named Felton, who blamed Buckingham in respect to some real or imaginary grievance. Felton had his revenge by assassinating Buckingham in the High Street, on August 22nd, 1628. Felton was hanged at Tyburn. The monument to the Duke of Buckingham consists of an urn, said to contain his heart, surmounted by a phœnix. On each side are pyramids of martial weapons, etc., and above, angels supporting the arms of the house of Villiers. At the base, Fame is represented with her trumpet, and a heart in the hand of

Sincerity. In the marriage registry book of this church is the register of the marriage of Charles II. with the infanta of Portugal, on May 22nd, 1662. The document is written in letters of gold.

LANDPORT.

HERE is the Royal Portsmouth, Portsea and Gosport Hospital, a large and attractive Railway Station, and a People's Park.

SOUTHSEA.

A Hundred years ago there was scarcely a house here. Now it is a large watering place. There are streets of large shops, lodging houses, etc. In a niche over King's Terrace is a statue of George III. in his coronation robes. Southsea Castle on the beach, was mostly re-built about 1814, though the original was erected in 1539 by Henry VIII. It accommodates 200 men besides officers, and is strongly fortified. The Common is extensive, and is used for drill practice and reviews. There is a splendid pebble beach, and an esplanade here.

There are monuments and captured cannons on the promenade, which extends to one of the largest barracks in England—Eastney. From Lumps Fort, near, there is artillery practice. Fort Cumberland is beyond.

The South Parade pier was opened on Saturday, July 26th, 1879, by the Princess Edward of Saxe Weimar.   It is 600 feet long, and has an octagon shaped head 150 feet across.

The Clarence Esplanade Pier has a splendid concert hall, reading room, etc.

HISTORY OF PORTSMOUTH.

IN the year 501 a body of Saxons took possession of Portsea Island and district. Several of our Kings landed here at different times.   Richard I. established the borough in 1200.   In 1372 the French burnt Portsmouth, but it soon re-appeared, and was strongly fortified in the primitive style.   One of the finest armies ever raised in England was that by Henry III., which was assembled here in 1221.   In 1245 the French fought us off Spithead, and though we had the best of it, it was not a very decisive victory.   On our side the *Mary Rose* was sunk, and Sir George Carew and 600 men were drowned.   Our *Great Harry* also suffered.   The contest lasted two days.   A shock of earthquake was felt in Portsmouth and neighbourhood in 1750.   At the King's Bastion is a gun recovered from the wreck of the *Royal George* in 1782, described on page 16.   It is related that a sheep swam ashore with an infant on its back clutching the fleece with its tiny fingers, and thus escaped the watery grave to which so

many strong-limbed men succumbed   In 1839
the *Royal George* was successfully blown to pieces
with gunpowder, by Colonel Pasley, in order to
prevent accidents.   On May Day, 1795, the
Boyne, ninety-one tons, drifted from Spithead,
enveloped in flames, and when the fire reached
the magazine, blew up with a terrific explosion,
the guns of the ship going off as the fire reached
them.   The fire lasted from eleven until five
o'clock.   A dozen pilferers who lay alongside
the ship in its burning state, in order to strip
the copper from her sides, were killed when she
blew up. All her crew were saved.   A memorial
of Lord Nelson in the form of a lofty pillar, on
the summit of Portsdown Hill, and which can be
seen for miles around inland,   and by ships
approaching Spithead, eastward or westward,
was erected by the officers and men who fought
under Nelson, the greatest of British admirals,
at Trafalgar, October 19th, 1805, contributing
two days' pay.   The anchor of the *Victory* is to
be seen near Southsea Pier, at the spot from
which Nelson embarked for the last time.   The
first English fleet under steam started from
Portsmouth in 1852.   Leaving the naval and
coming to the literary, we may mention that
Charles Dickens was born at 387, Commercial-
road, Landport, and the house is still standing.
He was the son of John Dickens a clerk in the
pay office.

EXCURSION COACHES
ISLE OF WIGHT.

◆

The Publisher is not certain that these Coaches will run Daily. Enquire at the Piers and Booking Offices.

Ryde to Brading, Roman Villa, Sandown, Lake, Shanklin Chine Benchurch and Ventnor—10.30 a.m.

Ventnor to Bonchurch, Shanklin Chine, Lake, Sandown, Roman Villa, Brading and Ryde—3.30 a.m.

Ryde to Binstead, Wootton, Newport, and Carisbrooke—10.20 a.m., 2.15 p.m.

Carisbrooke to Newport, Wootton, Binstead and Ryde—4.0 and 4.45 p.m.

Ventnor to Newport—11.0 a.m.

Newport to Ventnor—4.0 p.m.

Newport to Freshwater—11.25 a.m.

Freshwater to Newport—4.0 p.m.

Ventnor to Freshwater, Alum Bay and Totland Bay—10.10 a.m.

Totland Bay, Alum Bay and Freshwater to Ventnor—3.30 p.m.

Sandown to Freshwater—9.50 a.m.

Freshwater to Sandown—4.0 p.m.

Ryde to Newport—10.15 a.m., and 2.15 p.m.

Newport to Ryde—12.0 a.m., and 5.0 p.m.

Ventnor to Blackgang—11.45 a.m., and 4.30 p.m.

Blackgang to Ventnor—10.0 a.m., and 3.0 p.m.

Ventnor to Niton—11.0 a.m.

Niton to Ventnor—10.15 a.m., and 3.15 p.m.

Omnibuses and Luggage Vans meet all Trains.

CARRIERS.

Ryde to Brading, Sandown and Shanklin, on Monday, Wednesday Thursday and Saturday, at 10 a.m.—Adams, 3, High-street.

Sea View to Ryde, passing through Spring Vale at 10 a.m.

Ryde Pier to Spring Vale and Sea View, at 3. 30 p.m.

St. Helens, Nettlestone and Spring Vale, to Ryde at 10 a.m.

Ryde Pier to Nettlestone and St. Helens, at 3 p.m.

Ryde to Bembridge, at 3 p.m.—Broomfield (Ryde Pier.)

NOW READY. 16th EDITION. 105th THOUSAND.
POST FREE OF AUTHOR. FIVE SHILLINGS.

The CURE of
CONSUMPTION,

By an Entirely New Remedy.

Containing also Chapters on the Cure of

CHRONIC BRONCHITIS,

ASTHMA & CATARRH.

Under this Treatment an incredible number of Cases pronounced incurable by the most Eminent Physicians have recovered.

BY EDWIN W. ALABONE, M.D. Pa. U.S.A., F.R.M.S.

LYNTON HOUSE, 12, HIGHBURY QUADRANT,
LONDON, N.

Late Consulting Physician to the Home for Reclaimed Females, the Lower Clapton Orphan Asylum, and the Clapton Dispensary.

Author of "The Curative Treatment of Consumption:" "Phthisis, its Diagnosis and Treatment:" "The Specific Treatment of Phthisis," &c.

A Small Edition of above will be forwarded on receipt of Six Stamps.

Ingram Content Group UK Ltd.
Milton Keynes UK
UKHW031045310323
419467UK00009B/404